Harvard
Business
Review

ON
LEADING THROUGH
CHANGE

THE HARVARD BUSINESS REVIEW PAPERBACK SERIES

The series is designed to bring today's managers and professionals the fundamental information they need to stay competitive in a fast-moving world. From the preeminent thinkers whose work has defined an entire field to the rising stars who will redefine the way we think about business, here are the leading minds and landmark ideas that have established the *Harvard Business Review* as required reading for ambitious businesspeople in organizations around the globe.

Other books in the series:

Other books in the series (continued):

Harvard Business Review on Decision Making

Harvard Business Review on Developing Leaders

Harvard Business Review on Doing Business in China

Harvard Business Review on Effective Communication

Harvard Business Review on Entrepreneurship

Harvard Business Review on Finding and Keeping the Best People

Harvard Business Review on the High-Performance Organization

Harvard Business Review on Innovation

Harvard Business Review on the Innovative Enterprise

Harvard Business Review on Knowledge Management

Harvard Business Review on Leadership

Harvard Business Review on Leadership at the Top

Harvard Business Review on Leadership in a Changed World

Harvard Business Review on Leading in Turbulent Times

Harvard Business Review on Managing Diversity

Harvard Business Review on Managing High-Tech Industries

Harvard Business Review on Managing People

Harvard Business Review on Managing Projects

Harvard Business Review on Managing Uncertainty

Harvard Business Review on Managing the Value Chain

Harvard Business Review on Managing Your Career

Harvard Business Review on Managing Yourself

Harvard Business Review on Marketing

Harvard Business Review on Measuring Corporate Performance

Harvard Business Review on Mergers and Acquisitions

Harvard Business Review on the Mind of the Leader

Harvard Business Review on Motivating People

Harvard Business Review on Negotiation and Conflict Resolution

Harvard Business Review on Nonprofits

Harvard Business Review

ON

LEADING THROUGH CHANGE

A HARVARD BUSINESS REVIEW PAPERBACK

The *Harvard Business Review* articles in this collection are available as
individual reprints. Discounts apply to quantity purchases. For information and ordering, please contact Customer Service, Harvard Business
School Publishing, Boston, MA 02163. Telephone: (617) 783-7500 or
(800) 988-0886, 8 A.M. to 6 P.M. Eastern Time, Monday through Friday.
Fax: (617) 783-7555, 24 hours a day. E-mail: custserv@hbsp.harvard.edu.

978-1-4221-0280-0 (ISBN 13)

Library of Congress Cataloging-in-Publication Data
Harvard business review on leading through change.
        p.   cm. — (The Harvard business review paperback series)
    Includes index.
    ISBN 1-4221-0280-7
    1. Organizational change.   2. Leadership   I. Harvard Business
School Press.   II. Harvard business review.   III. Series.
HD58.8.H36945   2006
658.4´06—dc22   2006010629

Contents

Harvard Business Review

ON

LEADING THROUGH
CHANGE

Leading Change

Why Transformation Efforts Fail

JOHN P. KOTTER

Executive Summary

IN THE PAST DECADE, the author has watched more than 100 companies try to remake themselves into better competitors. Their efforts have gone under many banners: total quality management, reengineering, right sizing, restructuring, cultural change, and turnarounds. In almost every case, the goal has been the same: to cope with a new, more challenging market by changing how business is conducted.

A few of those efforts have been very successful. A few have been utter failures. Most fall somewhere in between, with a distinct tilt toward the lower end of the scale. The lessons that can be learned will be relevant to more and more organizations as the business environment becomes increasingly competitive in the coming decade.

One lesson is that change involves numerous phases that, together, usually take a long time. Skipping steps creates only an illusion of speed and never produces a satisfying result. A second lesson is that critical mistakes in any of the phases can have a devastating impact, slowing momentum and negating previous gains. Kotter's lessons are instructive, for even the most capable managers often make at least one big error.

OVER THE PAST DECADE, I have watched more than 100 companies try to remake themselves into significantly better competitors. They have included large organizations (Ford) and small ones (Landmark Communications), companies based in the United States (General Motors) and elsewhere (British Airways), corporations that were on their knees (Eastern Airlines), and companies that were earning good money (Bristol-Myers Squibb). These efforts have gone under many banners: total quality management, reengineering, right sizing, restructuring, cultural change, and turnaround. But, in almost every case, the basic goal has been the same: to make fundamental changes in how business is conducted in order to help cope with a new, more challenging market environment.

A few of these corporate change efforts have been very successful. A few have been utter failures. Most fall somewhere in between, with a distinct tilt toward the lower end of the scale. The lessons that can be drawn are interesting and will probably be relevant to even more organizations in the increasingly competitive business environment of the coming decade.

The most general lesson to be learned from the more successful cases is that the change process goes through a series of phases that, in total, usually require a considerable length of time. Skipping steps creates only the illusion of speed and never produces a satisfying result. A second very general lesson is that critical mistakes in any of the phases can have a devastating impact, slowing momentum and negating hard-won gains. Perhaps because we have relatively little experience in renewing organizations, even very capable people often make at least one big error.

Error #1: Not Establishing a Great Enough Sense of Urgency

Most successful change efforts begin when some individuals or some groups start to look hard at a company's competitive situation, market position, technological trends, and financial performance. They focus on the potential revenue drop when an important patent expires, the five-year trend in declining margins in a core business, or an emerging market that everyone seems to be ignoring. They then find ways to communicate this information broadly and dramatically, especially with respect to crises, potential crises, or great opportunities that are very timely. This first step is essential because just getting a transformation program started requires the aggressive cooperation of many individuals. Without motivation, people won't help and the effort goes nowhere.

Compared with other steps in the change process, phase one can sound easy. It is not. Well over 50% of the companies I have watched fail in this first phase. What are the reasons for that failure? Sometimes executives underestimate how hard it can be to drive people out of their comfort zones. Sometimes they grossly overestimate how successful they have already been in increasing urgency. Sometimes they lack patience: "Enough with the preliminaries; let's get on with it." In many cases, executives become paralyzed by the downside possibilities. They worry that employees with seniority will become defensive, that morale will drop, that events will spin out of control, that short-term business results will be jeopardized, that the stock will sink, and that they will be blamed for creating a crisis.

A paralyzed senior management often comes from having too many managers and not enough leaders. Management's mandate is to minimize risk and to keep the current system operating. Change, by definition, requires creating a new system, which in turn always demands leadership. Phase one in a renewal process typically goes nowhere until enough real leaders are promoted or hired into senior-level jobs.

Transformations often begin, and begin well, when an organization has a new head who is a good leader and who sees the need for a major change. If the renewal target is the entire company, the CEO is key. If change is needed in a division, the division general manager is key. When these individuals are not new leaders, great leaders, or change champions, phase one can be a huge challenge.

Bad business results are both a blessing and a curse in the first phase. On the positive side, losing money does catch people's attention. But it also gives less maneuvering room. With good business results, the opposite is true: convincing people of the need for change is much harder, but you have more resources to help make changes.

But whether the starting point is good performance or bad, in the more successful cases I have witnessed, an individual or a group always facilitates a frank discussion of potentially unpleasant facts: about new competition, shrinking margins, decreasing market share, flat earnings, a lack of revenue growth, or other relevant indices of a declining competitive position. Because there seems to be an almost universal human tendency to shoot the bearer of bad news, especially if the head of the organization is not a change champion, executives in these companies often rely on outsiders to bring unwanted information. Wall Street analysts, customers, and consultants can all be helpful in this regard. The purpose of all this activity, in the words of one former CEO of a large European company, is "to make the status quo seem more dangerous than launching into the unknown."

In a few of the most successful cases, a group has manufactured a crisis. One CEO deliberately engineered the largest accounting loss in the company's history, creating huge pressures from Wall Street in the process. One division president commissioned first-ever customer-satisfaction surveys, knowing full well that the results would be terrible. He then made these findings public. On the surface, such moves can look unduly risky. But there is also risk in playing it too safe: when the urgency rate is not pumped up enough, the transformation process cannot succeed and the long-term future of the organization is put in jeopardy.

When is the urgency rate high enough? From what I have seen, the answer is when about 75% of a company's management is honestly convinced that business-as-usual is totally unacceptable. Anything less can produce very serious problems later on in the process.

Error #2: Not Creating a Powerful Enough Guiding Coalition

Major renewal programs often start with just one or two people. In cases of successful transformation efforts, the leadership coalition grows and grows over time. But whenever some minimum mass is not achieved early in the effort, nothing much worthwhile happens.

It is often said that major change is impossible unless the head of the organization is an active supporter. What I am talking about goes far beyond that. In successful transformations, the chairman or president or division general manager, plus another 5 or 15 or 50 people, come together and develop a shared commitment to excellent performance through renewal. In my experience, this group never includes all of the company's most senior executives because some people just won't buy in, at least not at first. But in the most successful cases, the coalition is always pretty powerful—in terms of titles, information and expertise, reputations and relationships.

In both small and large organizations, a successful guiding team may consist of only three to five people during the first year of a renewal effort. But in big companies, the coalition needs to grow to the 20 to 50 range before much progress can be made in phase three and beyond. Senior managers always form the core of the group. But sometimes you find board members, a representative from a key customer, or even a powerful union leader.

Because the guiding coalition includes members who are not part of senior management, it tends to operate outside of the normal hierarchy by definition. This can be awkward, but it is clearly necessary. If the existing hierarchy were working well, there would be no need for a major transformation. But since the current system is not working, reform generally demands activity outside of formal boundaries, expectations, and protocol.

A high sense of urgency within the managerial ranks helps enormously in putting a guiding coalition together. But more is usually required. Someone needs to get these people together, help them develop a shared assessment of their company's problems and opportunities, and create a minimum level of trust and communication. Off-site retreats, for two or three days, are one popular vehicle for accomplishing this task. I have seen many groups of 5 to 35 executives attend a series of these retreats over a period of months.

Companies that fail in phase two usually underestimate the difficulties of producing change and thus the importance of a powerful guiding coalition. Sometimes they have no history of teamwork at the top and therefore undervalue the importance of this type of coalition. Sometimes they expect the team to be led by a staff executive from human resources, quality, or strategic planning instead of a key line manager. No matter how capable or dedicated the staff head, groups without strong line leadership never achieve the power that is required.

Efforts that don't have a powerful enough guiding coalition can make apparent progress for a while. But, sooner or later, the opposition gathers itself together and stops the change.

Error #3: Lacking a Vision

In every successful transformation effort that I have seen, the guiding coalition develops a picture of the future that is relatively easy to communicate and appeals to customers, stockholders, and employees. A vision always goes beyond the numbers that are typically found in five-year plans. A vision says something that helps clarify the direction in which an organization needs to move. Sometimes the first draft comes mostly from a single individual. It is usually a bit blurry, at least initially. But after the coalition works at it for 3 or 5 or even 12 months, something much better emerges through their tough analytical thinking and a little dreaming. Eventually, a strategy for achieving that vision is also developed.

In one midsize European company, the first pass at a vision contained two-thirds of the basic ideas that were in the final product. The concept of global reach was in the initial version from the beginning. So was the idea of becoming preeminent in certain businesses. But one central idea in the final version—getting out of low value-added activities—came only after a series of discussions over a period of several months.

Without a sensible vision, a transformation effort can easily dissolve into a list of confusing and incompatible projects that can take the organization in the wrong direction or nowhere at all. Without a sound vision, the reengineering project in the accounting department, the new 360-degree performance appraisal from the human resources department, the plant's quality program, the cultural change project in the sales force will not add up in a meaningful way.

In failed transformations, you often find plenty of plans and directives and programs, but no vision. In one case, a company gave out four-inch-thick notebooks describing its change effort. In mind-numbing detail, the books spelled out procedures, goals, methods, and deadlines. But nowhere was there a clear and compelling statement of where all this was leading. Not surprisingly, most of the employees with whom I talked were either confused or alienated. The big, thick books did not rally them together or inspire change. In fact, they probably had just the opposite effect.

In a few of the less successful cases that I have seen, management had a sense of direction, but it was too complicated or blurry to be useful. Recently, I asked an executive in a midsize company to describe his vision and received in return a barely comprehensible 30-minute lecture. Buried in his answer were the basic elements of a sound vision. But they were buried—deeply.

A useful rule of thumb: if you can't communicate the vision to someone in five minutes or less and get a reaction that signifies both understanding and interest, you are not yet done with this phase of the transformation process.

Error #4: Undercommunicating the Vision by a Factor of Ten

I've seen three patterns with respect to communication, all very common. In the first, a group actually does develop a pretty good transformation vision and then proceeds to communicate it by holding a single meeting or sending out a single communication. Having used about .0001% of the yearly intracompany communication, the group is startled that few people seem to understand the new approach. In the second pattern, the head of the organization spends a considerable amount of time making speeches to employee groups, but most people still don't get it (not surprising, since vision captures only .0005% of the total yearly communication). In the third pattern, much more effort goes into newsletters and speeches, but some very visible senior executives still behave in ways that are antithetical to the vision. The net result is that cynicism among the troops goes up, while belief in the communication goes down.

Transformation is impossible unless hundreds or thousands of people are willing to help, often to the point of making short-term sacrifices. Employees will not make sacrifices, even if they are unhappy with the status quo, unless they believe that useful change is possible.

Without credible communication, and a lot of it, the hearts and minds of the troops are never captured.

This fourth phase is particularly challenging if the short-term sacrifices include job losses. Gaining understanding and support is tough when downsizing is a part of the vision. For this reason, successful visions usually include new growth possibilities and the commitment to treat fairly anyone who is laid off.

Executives who communicate well incorporate messages into their hour-by-hour activities. In a routine discussion about a business problem, they talk about how proposed solutions fit (or don't fit) into the bigger picture. In a regular performance appraisal, they talk about how the employee's behavior helps or undermines the vision. In a review of a division's quarterly performance, they talk not only about the numbers but also about how the division's executives are contributing to the transformation. In a routine Q&A with employees at a company facility, they tie their answers back to renewal goals.

In more successful transformation efforts, executives use all existing communication channels to broadcast the vision. They turn boring and unread company newsletters into lively articles about the vision. They take ritualistic and tedious quarterly management meetings and turn them into exciting discussions of the transformation. They throw out much of the company's generic management education and replace it with courses that focus on business problems and the new vision. The guiding principle is simple: use every possible channel, especially those that are being wasted on nonessential information.

Perhaps even more important, most of the executives I have known in successful cases of major change learn to "walk the talk." They consciously attempt to become a living symbol of the new corporate culture. This is often not easy. A 60-year-old plant manager who has spent precious little time over 40 years thinking about customers will not suddenly behave in a customer-oriented way. But I have witnessed just such a person change, and change a great deal. In that case, a high level of urgency helped. The fact that the man was a part of the guiding coalition and the vision-creation team also helped. So did all the communication, which kept reminding him of the desired behavior, and all the feedback from his peers and subordinates, which helped him see when he was not engaging in that behavior.

Communication comes in both words and deeds, and the latter are often the most powerful form. Nothing undermines change more than behavior by important individuals that is inconsistent with their words.

Error #5: Not Removing Obstacles to the New Vision

Successful transformations begin to involve large numbers of people as the process progresses. Employees are emboldened to try new approaches, to develop new ideas, and to provide leadership. The only constraint is that the actions fit within the broad parameters of the overall vision. The more people involved, the better the outcome.

To some degree, a guiding coalition empowers others to take action simply by successfully communicating the new direction. But communication is never sufficient by itself. Renewal also requires the removal of obstacles. Too often, an employee understands the new vision and wants to help make it happen. But an elephant appears to be blocking the path. In some cases, the elephant is in the person's head, and the challenge is to convince the individual that no external obstacle exists. But in most cases, the blockers are very real.

Sometimes the obstacle is the organizational structure: narrow job categories can seriously undermine efforts to increase productivity or make it very difficult even to think about customers. Sometimes compensation or performance-appraisal systems make people choose between the new vision and their own self-interest. Perhaps worst of all are bosses who refuse to change and who make demands that are inconsistent with the overall effort.

One company began its transformation process with much publicity and actually made good progress through the fourth phase. Then the change effort ground to a halt because the officer in charge of the company's largest division was allowed to undermine most of the new initiatives. He paid lip service to the process but did not change his behavior or encourage his managers to change. He did not reward the unconventional ideas called for in the vision. He allowed human resource systems to remain intact even when they were clearly inconsistent with the new ideals. I think the officer's motives were complex. To some degree, he did not believe the company needed major change. To some degree, he felt personally threatened by all the change. To some degree, he was afraid that he could not produce both change and the expected operating profit. But despite the fact that they backed the renewal effort, the other officers did virtually nothing to stop the one blocker. Again, the reasons were complex. The company had no history of confronting problems like this. Some people were afraid of the officer. The CEO was concerned that he might lose a talented executive. The net result was disastrous. Lower level managers concluded that senior management had lied to them about their commitment to renewal, cynicism grew, and the whole effort collapsed.

In the first half of a transformation, no organization has the momentum, power, or time to get rid of all obstacles. But the big ones must be confronted and removed. If the blocker is a person, it is important that he or she be treated fairly and in a way that is consistent with the new vision. But action is essential, both to empower others and to maintain the credibility of the change effort as a whole.

Error #6: Not Systematically Planning for and Creating Short-Term Wins

Real transformation takes time, and a renewal effort risks losing momentum if there are no short-term goals to meet and celebrate. Most people won't go on the long march unless they see compelling evidence within 12 to 24 months that the journey is producing expected results. Without short-term wins, too many people give up or actively join the ranks of those people who have been resisting change.

One to two years into a successful transformation effort, you find quality beginning to go up on certain indices or the decline in net income stopping. You find some successful new product introductions or an upward shift in market share. You find an impressive productivity improvement or a statistically higher customer-satisfaction rating. But whatever the case, the win is unambiguous. The result is not just a judgment call that can be discounted by those opposing change.

Creating short-term wins is different from hoping for short-term wins. The latter is passive, the former active. In a successful transformation, managers actively look for ways to obtain clear performance improvements, establish goals in the yearly planning system, achieve the objectives, and reward the people involved with recognition, promotions, and even money. For example, the guiding coalition at a U.S. manufacturing company produced a highly visible and successful new product introduction about 20 months after the start of its renewal effort. The new product was selected about six months into the effort because it met multiple criteria: it could be designed and launched in a relatively short period; it could be handled by a small team of people who were devoted to the new vision; it had upside potential; and the new product-development team could operate outside the established departmental structure without practical problems. Little was left to chance, and the win boosted the credibility of the renewal process.

Managers often complain about being forced to produce short-term wins, but I've found that pressure can be a useful element in a change effort. When it becomes clear to people that major change will take a long time, urgency levels can drop. Commitments to produce short-term wins help keep the urgency level up and force detailed analytical thinking that can clarify or revise visions.

Error #7: Declaring Victory Too Soon

After a few years of hard work, managers may be tempted to declare victory with the first clear performance improvement. While celebrating a win is fine, declaring the war won can be catastrophic. Until changes sink deeply into a company's culture, a process that can take five to ten years, new approaches are fragile and subject to regression.

In the recent past, I have watched a dozen change efforts operate under the reengineering theme. In all but two cases, victory was declared and the expensive consultants were paid and thanked when the first major project was completed after two to three years. Within two more years, the useful changes that had been introduced slowly disappeared. In two of the ten cases, it's hard to find any trace of the reengineering work today.

Over the past 20 years, I've seen the same sort of thing happen to huge quality projects, organizational development efforts, and more. Typically, the problems start early in the process: the urgency level is not intense enough, the guiding coalition is not powerful enough, and the vision is not clear enough. But it is the premature victory celebration that kills momentum. And then the powerful forces associated with tradition take over.

Ironically, it is often a combination of change initiators and change resistors that creates the premature victory celebration. In their enthusiasm over a clear sign of progress, the initiators go overboard. They are then joined by resistors, who are quick to spot any opportunity to stop change. After the celebration is over, the resistors point to the victory as a sign that the war has been won and the troops should be sent home. Weary troops allow themselves to be convinced that they won. Once home, the foot soldiers are reluctant to climb back on the ships. Soon thereafter, change comes to a halt, and tradition creeps back in.

Instead of declaring victory, leaders of successful efforts use the credibility afforded by short-term wins to tackle even bigger problems. They go after systems and structures that are not consistent with the transformation vision and have not been confronted before. They pay great attention to who is promoted, who is hired, and how people are developed. They include new reengineering projects that are even bigger in scope than the initial ones. They understand that renewal efforts take not months but years. In fact, in one of the most successful transformations that I have ever seen, we quantified the amount of change that occurred each year over a seven-year period. On a scale of one (low) to ten (high), year one received a two, year two a four, year three a three, year four a seven, year five an eight, year six a four, and year seven a two. The peak came in year five, fully 36 months after the first set of visible wins.

Error #8: Not Anchoring Changes in the Corporation's Culture

In the final analysis, change sticks when it becomes "the way we do things around here," when it seeps into the bloodstream of the corporate body. Until new behaviors are rooted in social norms and shared values, they are subject to degradation as soon as the pressure for change is removed.

Two factors are particularly important in institution-alizing change in corporate culture. The first is a conscious attempt to show people how the new approaches, behaviors, and attitudes have helped improve performance. When people are left on their own to make the connections, they sometimes create very inaccurate links. For example, because results improved while charismatic Harry was boss, the troops link his mostly idiosyncratic style with those results instead of seeing how their own improved customer service and productivity were instrumental. Helping people see the right connections requires communication. Indeed, one company was relentless, and it paid off enormously. Time was spent at every major management meeting to discuss why performance was increasing. The company newspaper ran article after article showing how changes had boosted earnings.

The second factor is taking sufficient time to make sure that the next generation of top management really does personify the new approach. If the requirements for promotion don't change, renewal rarely lasts. One bad succession decision at the top of an organization can undermine a decade of hard work. Poor succession decisions are possible when boards of directors are not an integral part of the renewal effort. In at least three instances I have seen, the champion for change was the retiring executive, and although his successor was not a resistor, he was not a change champion. Because the boards did not understand the transformations in any detail, they could not see that their choices were not good fits. The retiring executive in one case tried unsuccessfully to talk his board into a less seasoned candidate who better personified the transformation. In the other two cases, the CEOs did not resist the boards' choices, because they felt the transformation could not be undone by their successors. They were wrong. Within two years, signs of renewal began to disappear at both companies.

THERE ARE STILL more mistakes that people make, but these eight are the big ones. I realize that in a short article everything is made to sound a bit too simplistic. In reality, even successful change efforts are messy and full of surprises. But just as a relatively simple vision is needed to guide people through a major change, so a vision of the change process can reduce the error rate. And fewer errors can spell the difference between success and failure.

Eight Steps to Transforming Your Organization

1 Establishing a Sense of Urgency
- Examining market and competitive realities
- Identifying and discussing crises, potential crises, or major opportunities

2 Forming a Powerful Guiding Coalition
- Assembling a group with enough power to lead the change effort
- Encouraging the group to work together as a team

3 Creating a Vision
- Creating a vision to help direct the change effort
- Developing strategies for achieving that vision

4 Communicating the Vision
- Using every vehicle possible to communicate the new vision and strategies
- Teaching new behaviors by the example of the guiding coalition

5 Empowering Others to Act on the Vision
- Getting rid of obstacles to change
- Changing systems or structures that seriously undermine the vision
- Encouraging risk taking and nontraditional ideas, activities, and actions

6 Planning for and Creating Short-Term Wins
- Planning for visible performance improvements
- Creating those improvements
- Recognizing and rewarding employees involved in the improvements

7 Consolidating Improvements and Producing Still More Change
- Using increased credibility to change systems, structures, and policies that don't fit the vision
- Hiring, promoting, and developing employees who can implement the vision
- Reinvigorating the process with new projects, themes, and change agents

8 Institutionalizing New Approaches
- Articulating the connections between the new behaviors and corporate success
- Developing the means to ensure leadership development and succession

Originally published in March–April 1995
Reprint 95204

Tipping Point Leadership

W. CHAN KIM AND RENÉE MAUBORGNE

Executive Summary

WHEN WILLIAM BRATTON was appointed police commissioner of New York City in 1994, turf wars over juris-
diction and funding were rife and crime was out of control. Yet in less than two years, and without an increase in
his budget, Bratton turned New York into the safest large
city in the nation. And the NYPD was only the latest of
five law-enforcement agencies Bratton had turned
around. In each case, he succeeded in record time
despite limited resources, a demotivated staff, opposition
from powerful vested interests, and an organization
wedded to the status quo.

Bratton's turnarounds demonstrate what the authors
call tipping point leadership. The theory of tipping
points hinges on the insight that in any organization,
fundamental changes can occur quickly when the

19

beliefs and energies of a critical mass of people create an epidemic movement toward an idea.

Bratton begins by overcoming the cognitive hurdles that block organizations from recognizing the need for change. He does this by putting managers face-to-face with operational problems. Next, he manages around limitations on funds, staff, or equipment by concentrating resources on the areas that are most in need of change and that have the biggest payoffs. He meanwhile solves the motivation problem by singling out key influencers—people with disproportionate power due to their connections or persuasive abilities. Finally, he closes off resistance from powerful opponents.

Not every CEO has the personality to be a Bill Bratton, but his successes are due to much more than his personality. He relies on a remarkably consistent method that any manager looking to turn around an organization can use to overcome the forces of inertia and reach the tipping point.

IN FEBRUARY 1994, William Bratton was appointed police commissioner of New York City. The odds were against him. The New York Police Department, with a $2 billion budget and a workforce of 35,000 police officers, was notoriously difficult to manage. Turf wars over jurisdiction and funding were rife. Officers were underpaid relative to their counterparts in neighboring communities, and promotion seemed to bear little relationship to performance. Crime had gotten so far out of control that the press referred to the Big Apple as the Rotten Apple. Indeed, many social scientists had concluded, after three decades of increases, that New York City crime was impervious to police intervention. The best the police could do was react to crimes once they were committed.

Yet in less than two years, and without an increase in his budget, Bill Bratton turned New York into the safest large city in the nation. Between 1994 and 1996, felony crime fell 39%; murders, 50%; and theft, 35%. Gallup polls reported that public confidence in the NYPD jumped from 37% to 73%, even as internal surveys showed job satisfaction in the police department reaching an all-time high. Not surprisingly, Bratton's popularity soared, and in 1996, he was featured on the cover of *Time*. Perhaps most impressive, the changes have outlasted their instigator, implying a fundamental shift in the department's organizational culture and strategy. Crime rates have continued to fall: Statistics released in December 2002 revealed that New York's overall crime rate is the lowest among the 25 largest cities in the United States.

The NYPD turnaround would be impressive enough for any police chief. For Bratton, though, it is only the latest of no fewer than five successful turnarounds in a 20-year career in policing. In the hope that Bratton can repeat his New York and Boston successes, Los Angeles has recruited him to take on the challenge of turning around the LAPD. (For a summary of his achievements, see the exhibit "Bratton in Action.")

So what makes Bill Bratton tick? As management researchers, we have long been fascinated by what triggers high performance or suddenly brings an ailing organization back to life. In an effort to find the common elements underlying such leaps in performance, we have built a database of more than 125 business and

Bratton in Action

The New York Police Department was not Bill Bratton's first turnaround. The table describes his biggest challenges and achievements during his 20 years as a policy reformer.

Domain	Boston Police District 4	Massachusetts Bay Transit Authority (MBTA)	Boston Metropolitan Police ("The Mets")	New York Transit Police (NYTP)	New York Police Department (NYPD)
Years	1977–1982	1983–1986	1986–1990	1990–1992	1994-1996
Position	Sergeant, lieutenant	Superintendent	Superintendent	Chief of police	Commissioner
Setting	Assaults, drug dealing, prostitution, public drinking, and graffiti were endemic to the area. The Boston public shied away from attending baseball games and other events and from shopping in the Fenway neighborhood for fear of being robbed or attacked or having their cars stolen.	Subway crime had been on the rise for the past five years. The media dubbed the Boston subway the Terror Train. The *Boston Globe* published a series on police incompetence in the MBTA.	The Mets lacked modern equipment, procedures, and discipline. Physical facilities were crumbling. Accountability, discipline, and morale were low in the 600-person Mets workforce.	Crime had risen 25% per year in the past three years—twice the overall rate for the city. Subway use by the public had declined sharply; polls indicated that New Yorkers considered the subway the most dangerous place in the city. There were 170,000 fare evaders per day, costing the city $80 million annually.	The middle class was fleeing to the suburbs in search of a better quality of life. There was public despair in the face of the high crime rate. Crime was seen as part of a breakdown of social norms. The budget for policing was shrinking. The NYPD budget (aside from personnel) was being cut by 35%.

	MBTA	Metropolitan Police	NYC Transit Police	NYPD
			Aggressive panhandling and vandalism were endemic. More than 5,000 people were living in the subway system.	The staff was demoralized and relatively underpaid.
Results	Crime throughout the Fenway area was dramatically reduced. Tourists, residents, and investment returned as an entire area of the city rebounded. Crime on the MBTA decreased by 27%; arrests rose to 1,600 per year from 600. The MBTA police met more than 800 standards of excellence to be accredited by the National Commission on Accreditation for Police Agencies. It was only the 13th police department in the country to meet this standard. Equipment acquired during his tenure: 55 new midsize cars, new uniforms, and new logos. Ridership began to grow.	Employee morale rose as Bratton instilled accountability, protocol, and pride. In three years, the Metropolitan Police changed from a dispirited, do-nothing, reactive organization with a poor self-image and an even worse public image to a very proud, proactive department. Equipment acquired during his tenure: 100 new vehicles, a helicopter, and a state-of-the-art radio system.	In two years, Bratton reduced felony crime by 22%, with robberies down by 40%. Increased confidence in the subway led to increased ridership. Fare evasion was cut in half. Equipment acquired during his tenure: a state-of-the-art communication system, advanced handguns for officers, and new patrol cars (the number of cars doubled).	Overall crime fell by 17%. Felony crime fell by 39%. Murders fell by 50%. Theft fell by 35% (robberies were down by one-third, burglaries by one-quarter). There were 200,000 fewer victims a year than in 1990. By the end of Bratton's tenure, the NYPD had a 73% positive rating, up from 37% four years earlier.

nonbusiness organizations. Bratton first caught our attention in the early 1990s, when we heard about his turnaround of the New York Transit Police. Bratton was special for us because in all of his turnarounds, he succeeded in record time despite facing all four of the hurdles that managers consistently claim block high performance: an organization wedded to the status quo, limited resources, a demotivated staff, and opposition from powerful vested interests. If Bratton could succeed against these odds, other leaders, we reasoned, could learn a lot from him.

Over the years, through our professional and personal networks and the rich public information available on the police sector, we have systematically compared the strategic, managerial, and performance records of Bratton's turnarounds. We have followed up by interviewing the key players, including Bratton himself, as well as many other people who for professional—or sometimes personal—reasons tracked the events.

Our research led us to conclude that all of Bratton's turnarounds are textbook examples of what we call tipping point leadership. The theory of tipping points, which has its roots in epidemiology, is well known; it hinges on the insight that in any organization, once the beliefs and energies of a critical mass of people are engaged, conversion to a new idea will spread like an epidemic, bringing about fundamental change very quickly. The theory suggests that such a movement can be unleashed only by agents who make unforgettable and unarguable calls for change, who concentrate their resources on what really matters, who mobilize the commitment of the organization's key players, and who succeed in silencing the most vocal naysayers. Bratton did all of these things in all of his turnarounds.

Most managers only dream of pulling off the kind of performance leaps Bratton delivered. Even Jack Welch needed some ten years and tens of millions of dollars of restructuring and training to turn GE into the power-house it is today. Few CEOs have the time and money that Welch had, and most—even those attempting relatively mild change—are soon daunted by the scale of the hurdles they face. Yet we have found that the dream can indeed become a reality. For what makes Bratton's turnarounds especially exciting to us is that his approach to overcoming the hurdles standing in the way of high performance has been remarkably consistent. His successes, therefore, are not just a matter of personality but also of method, which suggests that they can be replicated. Tipping point leadership is learnable.

In the following pages, we'll lay out the approach that has enabled Bratton to overcome the forces of inertia and reach the tipping point. We'll show first how Bratton overcame the cognitive hurdles that block companies from recognizing the need for radical change. Then we'll describe how he successfully managed around the public sector's endemic constraints on resources, which he even turned to his advantage. In the third section, we'll explain how Bratton overcame the motivational hurdles that had discouraged and demoralized even the most eager police officers. Finally, we'll describe how Bratton neatly closed off potentially fatal resistance from vocal and powerful opponents. (For a graphic summary of the ideas expressed in this article, see the exhibit "Tipping Point Leadership at a Glance.")

Tipping Point Leadership at a Glance

Leaders like Bill Bratton use a four-step process to bring about rapid, dramatic, and lasting change with limited resources. The cognitive and resource hurdles shown here represent the obstacles that organizations face in reorienting and formulating strategy. The motivational and political hurdles prevent a strategy's rapid execution. Tipping all four hurdles leads to rapid strategy reorientation and execution. Overcoming these hurdles is, of course, a continuous process because the innovation of today soon becomes the conventional norm of tomorrow.

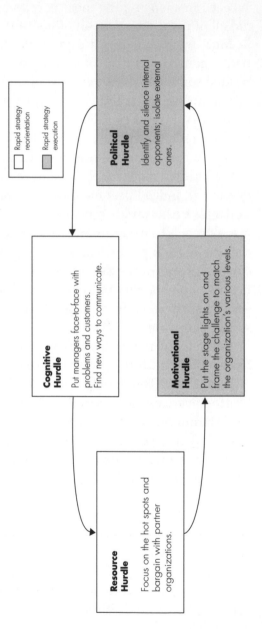

Break Through the Cognitive Hurdle

In many turnarounds, the hardest battle is simply getting people to agree on the causes of current problems and the need for change. Most CEOs try to make the case for change simply by pointing to the numbers and insisting that the company achieve better ones. But messages communicated through numbers seldom stick. To the line managers—the very people the CEO needs to win over—the case for change seems abstract and remote. Those whose units are doing well feel that the criticism is not directed at them, that the problem is top management's. Managers of poorly performing units feel that they have been put on notice—and people worried about job security are more likely to be scanning the job market than trying to solve the company's problems.

For all these reasons, tipping point leaders like Bratton do not rely on numbers to break through the organization's cognitive hurdles. Instead, they put their key managers face-to-face with the operational problems so that the managers cannot evade reality. Poor performance becomes something they witness rather than hear about. Communicating in this way means that the message—performance is poor and needs to be fixed—sticks with people, which is essential if they are to be convinced not only that a turnaround is necessary but that it is something they can achieve.

When Bratton first went to New York to head the transit police in April 1990, he discovered that none of the senior staff officers rode the subway. They commuted to work and traveled around in cars provided by the city. Comfortably removed from the facts of underground life—and reassured by statistics showing that only 3% of the city's major crimes were committed in the subway—

the senior managers had little sensitivity to riders' widespread concern about safety. In order to shatter the staff's complacency, Bratton began requiring that all transit police officials—beginning with himself—ride the subway to work, to meetings, and at night. It was many staff officers' first occasion in years to share the ordinary citizen's subway experience and see the situation their subordinates were up against: jammed turnstiles, aggressive beggars, gangs of youths jumping turnstiles and jostling people on the platforms, winos and homeless people sprawled on benches. It was clear that even if few major crimes took place in the subway, the whole place reeked of fear and disorder. With that ugly reality staring them in the face, the transit force's senior managers could no longer deny the need for a change in their policing methods.

Bratton uses a similar approach to help sensitize his superiors to his problems. For instance, when he was running the police division of the Massachusetts Bay Transit Authority (MBTA), which runs the Boston-area subway and buses, the transit authority's board decided to purchase small squad cars that would be cheaper to buy and run. Instead of fighting the decision, Bratton invited the MBTA's general manager for a tour of the district. He picked him up in a small car just like the ones that were to be ordered. He jammed the seats forward to let the general manager feel how little legroom a six-foot cop would have, then drove him over every pothole he could find. Bratton also put on his belt, cuffs, and gun for the trip so the general manager could see how little space there was for the tools of the officer's trade. After just two hours, the general manager wanted out. He said he didn't know how Bratton could stand being in such a cramped car for so long on his own—let alone if there were a criminal in the backseat. Bratton got the larger cars he wanted.

Bratton reinforces direct experiences by insisting that his officers meet the communities they are protecting. The feedback is often revealing. In the late 1970s, Boston's Police District 4, which included Symphony Hall, the Christian Science Mother Church, and other cultural institutions, was experiencing a surge in crime. The public was increasingly intimidated; residents were selling and leaving, pushing the community into a downward spiral. The Boston police performance statistics, however, did not reflect this reality. District 4 police, it seemed, were doing a splendid job of rapidly clearing 911 calls and tracking down perpetrators of serious crimes. To solve this paradox, Bratton had the unit organize community meetings in schoolrooms and civic centers so that citizens could voice their concerns to district sergeants and detectives. Obvious as the logic of this practice sounds, it was the first time in Boston's police history that anyone had attempted such an initiative— mainly because the practice up to that time had argued for detachment between police and the community in order to decrease the chances of police corruption.

The limitations of that practice quickly emerged. The meetings began with a show-and-tell by the officers: This is what we are working on and why. But afterward, when citizens were invited to discuss the issues that concerned them, a huge perception gap came to light. While the police officers took pride in solving serious offenses like grand larceny and murder, few citizens felt in any danger from these crimes. They were more troubled by constant minor irritants: prostitutes, panhandlers, broken-down cars left on the streets, drunks in the gutters, filth on the sidewalks. The town meetings quickly led to a complete overhaul of the police priorities for District 4. Bratton has used community meetings like this in every turnaround since.

Bratton's internal communications strategy also plays an important role in breaking through the cognitive hurdles. Traditionally, internal police communication is largely based on memos, staff bulletins, and other documents. Bratton knows that few police officers have the time or inclination to do more than throw these documents into the wastebasket. Officers rely instead on rumor and media stories for insights into what headquarters is up to. So Bratton typically calls on the help of expert communication outsiders. In New York, for instance, he recruited John Miller, an investigative television reporter known for his gutsy and innovative style, as his communication czar. Miller arranged for Bratton to communicate through video messages that were played at roll calls, which had the effect of bringing Bratton— and his opinions—closer to the people he had to win over. At the same time, Miller's journalistic savvy made it easier for the NYPD to ensure that press interviews and stories echoed the strong internal messages Bratton was sending.

Sidestep the Resource Hurdle

Once people in an organization accept the need for change and more or less agree on what needs to be done, leaders are often faced with the stark reality of limited resources. Do they have the money for the necessary changes? Most reformist CEOs do one of two things at this point. They trim their ambitions, dooming the company to mediocrity at best and demoralizing the workforce all over again, or they fight for more resources from their bankers and shareholders, a process that can take time and divert attention from the underlying problems.

That trap is completely avoidable. Leaders like Bratton know how to reach the organization's tipping point without extra resources. They can achieve a great deal with the resources they have. What they do is concentrate their resources on the places that are most in need of change and that have the biggest possible payoffs. This idea, in fact, is at the heart of Bratton's famous (and once hotly debated) philosophy of zero-tolerance policing.

Having won people over to the idea of change, Bratton must persuade them to take a cold look at what precisely is wrong with their operating practices. It is at this point that he turns to the numbers, which he is adept at using to force through major changes. Take the case of the New York narcotics unit. Bratton's predecessors had treated it as secondary in importance, partly because they assumed that responding to 911 calls was the top priority. As a result, less than 5% of the NYPD's manpower was dedicated to fighting narcotics crimes.

At an initial meeting with the NYPD's chiefs, Bratton's deputy commissioner of crime strategy, Jack Maple, asked people around the table for their estimates of the percentage of crimes attributable to narcotics use. Most said 50%; others, 70%; the lowest estimate was 30%. On that basis, a narcotics unit consisting of less than 5% of the police force was grossly understaffed, Maple pointed out. What's more, it turned out that the narcotics squad largely worked Monday through Friday, even though drugs were sold in large quantities—and drug-related crimes persistently occurred—on the weekends. Why the weekday schedule? Because it had always been done that way; it was an unquestioned modus operandi. Once these

facts were presented, Bratton's call for a major realloca-
tion of staff and resources within the NYPD was quickly
accepted.

A careful examination of the facts can also reveal
where changes in key policies can reduce the need for
resources, as Bratton demonstrated during his tenure as
chief of New York's transit police. His predecessors had
lobbied hard for the money to increase the number of
subway cops, arguing that the only way to stop muggers
was to have officers ride every subway line and patrol
each of the system's 700 exits and entrances. Bratton, by
contrast, believed that subway crime could be resolved
not by throwing more resources at the problem but by
better targeting those resources. To prove the point, he
had members of his staff analyze where subway crimes
were being committed. They found that the vast majority
occurred at only a few stations and on a couple of lines,
which suggested that a targeted strategy would work
well. At the same time, he shifted more of the force out of
uniform and into plain clothes at the hot spots. Crimi-
nals soon realized that an absence of uniforms did not
necessarily mean an absence of cops.

Distribution of officers was not the only problem.
Bratton's analysis revealed that an inordinate amount of
police time was wasted in processing arrests. It took an
officer up to 16 hours per arrest to book the suspect and
file papers on the incident. What's more, the officers so
hated the bureaucratic process that they avoided making
arrests in minor cases. Bratton realized that he could
dramatically increase his available policing resources—
not to mention the officers' motivation—if he could
somehow improvise around this problem. His solution
was to park "bust buses"—old buses converted into
arrest-processing centers—around the corner from tar-

geted subway stations. Processing time was cut from 16 hours to just one. Innovations like that enabled Bratton to dramatically reduce subway crime—even without an increase in the number of officers on duty at any given time. (The exhibit "The Strategy Canvas of Transit: How Bratton Refocused Resources" illustrates how radically Bratton refocused the transit police's resources.)

Bratton's drive for data-driven policing solutions led to the creation of the famous Compstat crime database. The database, used to identify hot spots for intense police intervention, captures weekly crime and arrest activity—including times, locations, and associated enforcement activities—at the precinct, borough, and city levels. The Compstat reports allowed Bratton and the entire police department to easily discern established and emerging hot spots for efficient resource targeting and retargeting.

In addition to refocusing the resources he already controls, Bratton has proved adept at trading resources he doesn't need for those he does. The chiefs of public-sector organizations are reluctant to advertise excess resources, let alone lend them to other agencies, because acknowledged excess resources tend to get reallocated. So over time, some organizations end up well endowed with resources they don't need—even if they are short of others. When Bratton took over as chief of the transit police, for example, his general counsel and policy adviser, Dean Esserman, now police chief of Providence, Rhode Island, discovered that the transit unit had more unmarked cars than it needed but was starved of office space. The New York Division of Parole, on the other hand, was short of cars but had excess office space. Esserman and Bratton offered the obvious trade. It was gratefully accepted by the parole division, and transit

The Strategy Canvas of Transit: How Bratton Refocused Resources

In comparing strategies across companies, we like to use a tool we call the strategy canvas, which highlights differences in strategies and resource allocation. The strategy canvas shown here compares the strategy and allocation of resources of the New York Transit Police before and after Bill Bratton's appointment as chief. The vertical axis shows the relative level of resource allocation. The horizontal axis shows the various elements of strategy in which the investments were made. Although a dramatic shift in resource allocation occurred and performance rose dramatically, overall investment of resources remained more or less constant. Bratton did this by de-emphasizing or virtually eliminating some traditional features of transit police work while increasing emphasis on others or creating new ones. For example, he was able to reduce the time police officers spent processing suspects by introducing mobile processing centers known as "bust buses."

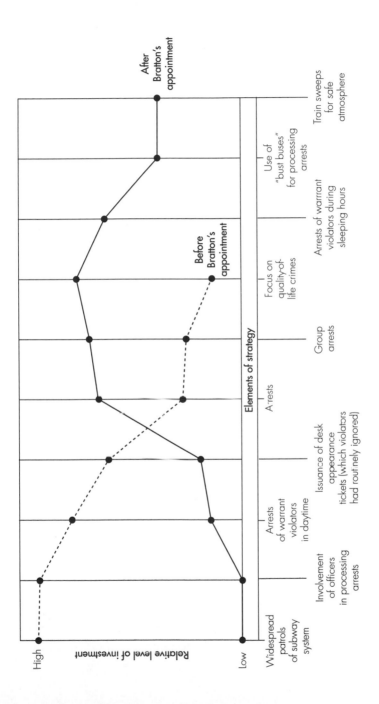

officials were delighted to get the first floor of a prime downtown building. The deal stoked Bratton's credibility within the organization, which would make it easier for him to introduce more fundamental changes later, and it marked him, to his political bosses, as a man who could solve problems.

Jump the Motivational Hurdle

Alerting employees to the need for change and identifying how it can be achieved with limited resources are necessary for reaching an organization's tipping point. But if a new strategy is to become a movement, employees must not only recognize what needs to be done, they must also want to do it. Many CEOs recognize the importance of getting people motivated to make changes, but they make the mistake of trying to reform incentives throughout the whole organization. That process takes a long time to implement and can prove very expensive, given the wide variety of motivational needs in any large company.

One way Bratton solves the motivation problem is by singling out the key influencers—people inside or outside the organization with disproportionate power due to their connections with the organization, their ability to persuade, or their ability to block access to resources. Bratton recognizes that these influencers act like kingpins in bowling: When you hit them just right, all the pins topple over. Getting the key influencers motivated frees an organization from having to motivate everyone, yet everyone in the end is touched and changed. And because most organizations have relatively small numbers of key influencers, and those people tend to share common problems and concerns, it is relatively easy for CEOs to identify and motivate them.

Bratton's approach to motivating his key influencers is to put them under a spotlight. Perhaps his most significant reform of the NYPD's operating practices was instituting a semiweekly strategy review meeting that brought the top brass together with the city's 76 precinct commanders. Bratton had identified the commanders as key influential people in the NYPD, because each one directly managed 200 to 400 officers. Attendance was mandatory for all senior staff, including three-star chiefs, deputy commissioners, and borough chiefs. Bratton was there as often as possible.

At the meetings, which took place in an auditorium at the police command center, a selected precinct commander was called before a panel of the senior staff (the selected officer was given only two days' notice, in order to keep all the commanders on their toes). The commander in the spotlight was questioned by both the panel and other commanders about the precinct's performance. He or she was responsible for explaining projected maps and charts that showed, based on the Compstat data, the precinct's patterns of crimes and when and where the police responded. The commander would be required to provide a detailed explanation if police activity did not mirror crime spikes and would also be asked how officers were addressing the precinct's issues and why performance was improving or deteriorating. The meetings allowed Bratton and his senior staff to carefully monitor and assess how well commanders were motivating and managing their people and how well they were focusing on strategic hot spots.

The meetings changed the NYPD's culture in several ways. By making results and responsibilities clear to everyone, the meetings helped to introduce a culture of performance. Indeed, a photo of the commander who was about to be grilled appeared on the front page of the handout that each meeting participant received, emphasizing that the commander was accountable for the precinct's results. An incompetent commander could no longer cover up his failings by blaming his precinct's results on the shortcomings of neighboring precincts, because his neighbors were in the room and could respond. By the same token, the meetings gave high achievers a chance to be recognized both for making improvements in their own precincts and for helping other commanders. The meetings also allowed police leaders to compare notes on their experiences; before Bratton's arrival, precinct commanders hardly ever got together as a group. Over time, this management style filtered down through the ranks, as the precinct commanders tried out their own versions of Bratton's meetings. With the spotlight shining brightly on their performance, the commanders were highly motivated to get all the officers under their control marching to the new strategy.

The great challenges in applying this kind of motivational device, of course, are ensuring that people feel it is based on fair processes and seeing to it that they can draw lessons from both good and bad results. Doing so increases the organization's collective strength and everyone's chance of winning. Bratton addresses the issue of fair process by engaging all key influencers in the procedures, setting clear performance expectations, and explaining why these strategy meetings, for example, are essential for fast execution of policy. He addresses the issue of learning by insisting that the team of top brass play an active role in meetings and by being an active moderator himself. Precinct commanders can talk about their achievements or failures without feeling that they are showing off or being shown up. Successful commanders aren't seen as bragging, because it's clear to everyone that they were asked by Bratton's top team to show, in detail, how they achieved their successes. And for commanders on the receiving end, the sting of having to be taught a lesson by a colleague is mitigated, at least, by their not having to suffer the indignity of asking for it. Bratton's popularity soared when he created a humorous video satirizing the grilling that precinct commanders were given; it showed the cops that he understood just how much he was asking of them.

Bratton also uses another motivational lever: framing the reform challenge itself. Framing the challenge is one of the most subtle and sensitive tasks of the tipping point leader; unless people believe that results are attainable, a turnaround is unlikely to succeed. On the face of it, Bratton's goal in New York was so ambitious as to be scarcely believable. Who would believe that the city could be made one of the safest in the country? And who would want to invest time and energy in chasing such an impossible dream?

To make the challenge seem manageable, Bratton framed it as a series of specific goals that officers at different levels could relate to. As he put it, the challenge the NYPD faced was to make the streets of New York safe "block by block, precinct by precinct, and borough by borough." Thus framed, the task was both all encompassing and doable. For the cops on the street, the challenge was making their beats or blocks safe—no more. For the commanders, the challenge was making their

precincts safe—no more. Borough heads also had a concrete goal within their capabilities: making their bor-
oughs safe—no more. No matter what their positions,
officers couldn't say that what was being asked of them
was too tough. Nor could they claim that achieving it
was out of their hands. In this way, responsibility for the
turnaround shifted from Bratton to each of the thousands of police officers on the force.

Knock Over the Political Hurdle

Organizational politics is an inescapable reality in public
and corporate life, a lesson Bratton learned the hard way.
In 1980, at age 34 one of the youngest lieutenants in
Boston's police department, he had proudly put up a
plaque in his office that said: "Youth and skill will win out
every time over age and treachery." Within just a few
months, having been shunted into a dead-end position
due to a mixture of office politics and his own brashness,
Bratton took the sign down. He never again forgot the
importance of understanding the plotting, intrigue,
and politics involved in pushing through change. Even
if an organization has reached the tipping point, powerful vested interests will resist the impending reforms.
The more likely change becomes, the more fiercely and
vocally these negative influencers—both internal and
external—will fight to protect their positions, and their
resistance can seriously damage, even derail, the reform
process.

  Bratton anticipates these dangers by identifying and
silencing powerful naysayers early on. To that end, he
always ensures that he has a respected senior insider on
the top team. At the NYPD, for instance, Bratton ap-

pointed John Timoney, now Miami's police commissioner, as his number two. Timoney was a cop's cop, respected and feared for his dedication to the NYPD and for the more than 60 decorations he had received. Twenty years in the ranks had taught him who all the key players were and how they played the political game. One of the first tasks Timoney carried out was to report to Bratton on the likely attitudes of the top staff toward Bratton's concept of zero-tolerance policing, identifying those who would fight or silently sabotage the new initiatives. This led to a dramatic changing of the guard.

Of course, not all naysayers should face the ultimate sanction—there might not be enough people left to man the barricades. In many cases, therefore, Bratton silences opposition by example and indisputable fact. For instance, when first asked to compile detailed crime maps and information packages for the strategy review meetings, most precinct commanders complained that the task would take too long and waste valuable police time that could be better spent fighting crime. Anticipating this argument, deputy commissioner Jack Maple set up a reporting system that covered the city's most crime-ridden areas. Operating the system required no more than 18 minutes a day, which worked out, as he told the precinct commanders, to less than 1% of the average precinct's workload. Try to argue with that.

Often the most serious opposition to reform comes from outside. In the public sector, as in business, an organization's change of strategy has an impact on other organizations—partners and competitors alike. The change is likely to be resisted by those players if they are happy with the status quo and powerful enough to protest the changes. Bratton's strategy for dealing with such opponents is to isolate them by building a broad coalition with the other independent powers in his realm. In New York, for example, one of the most serious threats to his reforms came from the city's courts, which were concerned that zero-tolerance policing would result in an enormous number of small-crimes cases clogging the court schedule.

To get past the opposition of the courts, Bratton solicited the support of no less a personage than the mayor, Rudolph Giuliani, who had considerable influence over the district attorneys, the courts, and the city jail on Rikers Island. Bratton's team demonstrated to the mayor that the court system had the capacity to handle minor "quality of life" crimes, even though doing so would presumably not be palatable for them.

The mayor decided to intervene. While conceding to the courts that a crackdown campaign would cause a short-term spike in court work, he also made clear that he and the NYPD believed it would eventually lead to a workload reduction for the courts. Working together in this way, Bratton and the mayor were able to maneuver the courts into processing quality-of-life crimes. Seeing that the mayor was aligned with Bratton, the courts appealed to the city's legislators, advocating legislation to exempt them from handling minor-crime cases on the grounds that such cases would clog the system and entail significant costs to the city. Bratton and the mayor, who were holding weekly strategy meetings, added another ally to their coalition by placing their case before the press, in particular the *New York Times*. Through a series of press conferences and articles and at every interview opportunity, the issue of zero tolerance was put at the front and center of public debate with a clear, simple message: If the courts did not help crack down on quality-of-life crimes, the city's crime rates would not improve. It was a matter not of saving dollars but of saving the city.

Bratton's alliance with the mayor's office and the city's leading media institution successfully isolated the courts. The courts could hardly be seen as publicly opposing an initiative that would not only make New York a more attractive place to live but would ultimately reduce the number of cases brought before them. With the mayor speaking aggressively in the press about the need to pursue quality-of-life crimes and the city's most respected—and liberal—newspaper giving credence to the policy, the costs of fighting Bratton's strategy were daunting. Thanks to this savvy politicking, one of Bratton's biggest battles was won, and the legislation was not enacted. The courts would handle quality-of-life crimes. In due course, the crime rates did indeed come tumbling down.

O<small>F COURSE</small>, Bill Bratton, like any leader, must share the credit for his successes. Turning around an organization as large and as wedded to the status quo as the NYPD requires a collective effort. But the tipping point would not have been reached without him—or another leader like him. And while we recognize that not every executive has the personality to be a Bill Bratton, there are many who have that potential once they know the formula for success. It is that formula that we have tried to present, and we urge managers who wish to turn their companies around, but have limited time and resources, to take note. By addressing the hurdles to tipping point change described in these pages, they will stand a chance of achieving the same kind of results for their shareholders as Bratton has delivered to the citizens of New York.

Originally published in April 2003
Reprint R0304D

Why Do Employees Resist Change?

PAUL STREBEL

Executive Summary

DESPITE THE BEST EFFORTS of senior executives, major change initiatives often fail. Those failures have at least one common root: Executives and employees see change differently. For senior managers, change means opportunity—both for the business and for themselves. But for many employees, change is seen as disruptive and intrusive.

To close this gap, says Paul Strebel, managers must reconsider their employees' "personal compacts"—the mutual obligations and commitments that exist between employees and the company. Personal compacts in all companies have three dimensions: formal, psychological, and social. Employees determine their responsibilities, their level of commitment to their work, and the company's values by asking questions along these dimensions. How a company answers them is the key to successful change.

Two case studies demonstrate the effectiveness of revising personal compacts. In the first, Strebel describes how the CEO of Philips Electronics, Jan Timmer, pulled the company back from the brink of bankruptcy by replacing a risk-averse culture with one in which employees were committed fully to the company's goals.

In the second, the author examines how Haruo Naito, the CEO of Eisai, a Japanese pharmaceutical company, anticipated potential crises and created the context for long-term change. Eisai's employees took the lead in revising their own personal compacts; as a result, the company accomplished a major strategic change. The message is clear. Whether facing an immediate crisis or pursuing a new long-term vision, leaders can overcome their employees' resistance to change by redefining their personal compacts.

CHANGE MANAGEMENT ISN'T WORKING as it should. In a telling statistic, leading practitioners of radical corporate reengineering report that success rates in *Fortune* 1,000 companies are well below 50%; some say they are as low as 20%. The scenario is all too familiar. Company leaders talk about total quality management, downsizing, or customer value. Determined managers follow up with plans for process improvements in customer service, manufacturing, and supply chain management, and for new organizations to fit the new processes. From subordinates, management looks for enthusiasm, acceptance, and commitment. But it gets something less. Communication breaks down, implementation plans miss their mark, and results fall short. This happens often enough that we have to ask why, and how we can avoid these failures.

In the Change Program at IMD, in which executives tackle actual change problems from their own companies, I have worked with more than 200 managers from 32 countries, all of whom are struggling to respond to the shocks of rapidly evolving markets and technology. Although each company's particular circumstances account for some of the problems, the widespread difficulties have at least one common root: Managers and employees view change differently. Both groups know that vision and leadership drive successful change, but far too few leaders recognize the ways in which individuals commit to change to bring it about. Top-level managers see change as an opportunity to strengthen the business by aligning operations with strategy, to take on new professional challenges and risks, and to advance their careers. For many employees, however, including middle managers, change is neither sought after nor welcomed. It is disruptive and intrusive. It upsets the balance.

Senior managers consistently misjudge the effect of this gap on their relationships with subordinates and on the effort required to win acceptance of change. To close the gap, managers at all levels must learn to see things differently. They must put themselves in their employees' shoes to understand how change looks from that perspective and to examine the terms of the "personal compacts" between employees and the company.

What Is a Personal Compact?

Employees and organizations have reciprocal obligations and mutual commitments, both stated and implied, that define their relationship. Those agreements are what I call personal compacts, and corporate change initiatives, whether proactive or reactive, alter their terms. Unless managers define new terms and persuade employees to accept them, it is unrealistic for managers to expect employees fully to buy into changes that alter the status quo. As results all too often prove, disaffected employees will undermine their managers' credibility and well-designed plans. However, I have observed initiatives in which personal compacts were successfully revised to support major change—although the revision process was not necessarily explicit or deliberate. Moreover, I have identified three major dimensions shared by compacts in all companies. These common dimensions are *formal, psychological,* and *social.*

The *formal* dimension of a personal compact is the most familiar aspect of the relationship between employees and their employers. For an employee, it captures the basic tasks and performance requirements for a job as defined by company documents such as job descriptions, employment contracts, and performance agreements. Business or budget plans lay out expectations of financial performance. In return for the commitment to perform, managers convey the authority and resources each individual needs to do his or her job. What isn't explicitly committed to in writing is usually agreed to orally. From an employee's point of view, personal commitment to the organization comes from understanding the answers to the following series of questions:

- What am I supposed to do for the organization?

- What help will I get to do the job?

- How and when will my performance be evaluated, and what form will the feedback take?

- What will I be paid, and how will pay relate to my performance evaluation?

Companies may differ in their approach to answering those questions, but most have policies and procedures that provide direction and guidelines to managers and employees. Nevertheless, a clear, accurate formal compact does not ensure that employees will be satisfied with their jobs or that they will make the personal commitment managers expect. Unfortunately, many managers stop here when anticipating how change will affect employees. In fact, performance along this dimension is tightly linked to the other two.

The *psychological* dimension of a personal compact addresses aspects of the employment relationship that are mainly implicit. It incorporates the elements of mutual expectation and reciprocal commitment that arise from feelings like trust and dependence between employee and employer. Though often unwritten, the psychological dimension underpins an employee's personal commitment to individual and company objectives. Managers expect employees to be loyal and willing to do whatever it takes to get the job done, and they routinely make observations and assumptions about the kind of commitment their employees display. The terms of a job description rarely capture the importance of commitment, but employees' behavior reflects their awareness of it. Employees determine their commitment to the organization along the psychological dimension of their personal compact by asking:

- How hard will I really have to work?

- What recognition, financial reward, or other personal satisfaction will I get for my efforts?

- Are the rewards worth it?

Individuals formulate responses to those questions in large part by evaluating their relationship with their boss. Their loyalty and commitment is closely connected to their belief in their manager's willingness to recognize a job well done, and not just with more money. In the context of a major change program, a manager's sensitivity to this dimension of his or her relationship with subordinates is crucial to gaining commitment to new goals and performance standards.

Employees gauge an organization's culture through the *social* dimension of their personal compacts. They note what the company says about its values in its mission statement and observe the interplay between company practices and management's attitude toward them. Perceptions about the company's main goals are tested when employees evaluate the balance between financial and nonfinancial objectives, and when they determine whether management practices what it preaches. They translate those perceptions about values into beliefs about how the company really works—about the unspoken rules that apply to career development, promotions, decision making, conflict resolution, resource allocation, risk sharing, and layoffs. Along the social dimension, an employee tries to answer these specific questions:

- Are my values similar to those of others in the organization?

- What are the real rules that determine who gets what in this company?

Alignment between a company's statements and management's behavior is the key to creating a context that evokes employee commitment along the social dimension. It is often the dimension of a personal compact that is undermined most in a change initiative when conflicts arise and communication breaks down. Moreover, it is the dimension along which management's credibility, once lost, is most difficult to recover.

Unrevised Personal Compacts Block Change

Looking through the lens of unrevised personal compacts, employees often misunderstand or, worse, ignore the implications of change for their individual commitments. At Philips Electronics, based in the Netherlands, employees' failure to understand changing circumstances drove the organization to the brink of bankruptcy.

In the early 1980s, Philips's reputation for engineering excellence and financial strength was unparalleled, and it was a prestigious company to work for. The company—which pioneered the development of the audio cassette, the video recorder, and the compact disc—recruited the best electrical engineers in the Netherlands.

Like many multidomestic European companies, Philips had a matrix structure in which strong country managers ran the international sales and marketing subsidiaries like fiefdoms. Local product divisions were organized separately, and competition for resources among the different business units was vigorous. Central control was anathema, but the size and complexity of headquarters in Eindhoven grew nevertheless.

At the same time, competition was intensifying. Despite its continued excellence in engineering innovation, Philips was having trouble getting new products to market in a timely way. Margins were squeezed as manufacturing costs slipped out of line in comparison with Sony's and Panasonic's, and market share started falling even in the company's northern European heartland, where Sony was rapidly taking over the leading position. During the 1980s, two successive CEOs, Wisse Dekkers and Cor van der Klugt, tried to redirect the company. Each, in his time, hammered home the problems that needed correcting: the pace and quality of product development, slow time to market, and high manufacturing costs. The two men communicated vigorously, reorganized, and set up task forces on change. In Philips's 1989 annual report, van der Klugt reported that he had redefined management responsibilities to give product divisions greater freedom to respond to competitive and market pressures. Yet the projected improvements in costs and market share did not materialize quickly enough. At the end of van der Klugt's tenure, Philips was facing the biggest operating loss in the company's history.

Why couldn't either of those seasoned professional managers deal with the changes in the competitive environment? They understood the problems, articulated the plans, and undertook the initiatives that we associate with change leadership. Yet each failed in his attempt to redirect the company in time because widespread employee support was missing. In fact, personal compacts in place at the time actually blocked change because there was little alignment between senior managers' statements and the practice and attitude of lower-level managers and their subordinates.

But the problem could have been predicted. During Philips's prosperous years, a tradition of lifelong employment was part of the company culture. Job security came in exchange for loyalty to the company and to individual managers. Informal rules and personal relationships dominated formal systems for performance evaluations and career advancement. Managers' job descriptions and position in the hierarchy set limits on their responsibilities, and operating outside those boundaries was discouraged. Subordinates weren't encouraged any differently. People weren't trying to meet challenges facing the company or even looking for personal growth. Position and perceived power in the company network determined who got what. And because seniority so directly affected an employee's career growth and level of compensation, workers had no incentive to work harder than people just above them or to exceed their boss's minimum expectations for performance.

Moreover, even when costs were demonstrably out of line and operating margins were declining, Philips had no effective mechanism for holding managers accountable for failing to achieve financial targets. Budget-to-actual variances were attributed to events outside the control of unit managers. And because of the limitations of financial reporting systems and a culture that encouraged loyalty over performance, no one was able to challenge this mind-set effectively.

None of that changed under Dekkers or van der Klugt. Managers and subordinates were not forced to understand how the changes essential to turning the company around would require them to take a fundamentally different view of their obligations. Neither Dekkers nor van der Klugt drove the process far enough to alter employees' perceptions and bring about revised personal compacts.

By the time Jan Timmer took over at Philips in May 1990, the company faced a crisis. Net operating income in the first quarter of 1990 was 6 million guilders compared with 223 million guilders the previous year, and the net operating loss for the year was projected by analysts at 1.2 billion guilders. Timmer was an insider from the consumer electronics division, where he had successfully stopped mounting operating losses. But the scale of

Timmer's challenge to turn the company around was matched by the pressure on him to deal quickly and effectively with the potentially crippling losses.

Orchestrating the Revision of Compacts

The revision of personal compacts occurs in three phases. First, leaders draw attention to the need to change and establish the context for revising compacts. Second, they initiate a process in which employees are able to revise and buy into new compact terms. Finally, they lock in commitments with new formal and informal rules. By approaching these phases systematically and creating explicit links between employees' commitments and the company's necessary change outcomes, managers dramatically improve the probability of hitting demanding targets. To lead Philips out of its crisis, Jan Timmer had to steer the company through those phases.

SHOCK TREATMENT AT PHILIPS

Although the competitive landscape around Philips had changed, the company and its employees had not. Employees' personal compacts favored maintaining the status quo, so resistance to change was imbedded in the culture. To achieve a turnaround, Timmer was going to have to reach deep into the organization and not only lead the initiative but also closely manage it. Getting people's attention was merely the first step. Persuading them to revise the terms of their personal compacts was a much bigger challenge.

Timmer's approach was a dramatic one; in fact, it was shock treatment. Shortly after becoming CEO in mid-1990, he invited the company's top 100 man-

agers to an off-site retreat at Philips's training center in
De Ruwenberg. There he explained the company's situation in stark terms: Its survival was in jeopardy. To reinforce the message, he handed out a hypothetical press
release stating that Philips was bankrupt. It was up to
the group in the room to bring the company back.
Everyone would have to contribute. Operation Centurion had begun and, with it, the end of life in the company as all those in the room had known it.

From the start, Timmer's terms for change were
tough and unambiguous, and those who didn't like them
were encouraged to leave. In Operation Centurion, Timmer captured the mind-set he wanted and created the
process he would use to focus managers' attention on the
new goals. Extending the metaphor, Timmer offered his
managers new personal contracts, which were like the
assignments given officers by their superiors in the
Roman army. In the ensuing Centurion Sessions, the
terms of these new compacts would begin to take shape.

Drawing on benchmarking data on best-in-class productivity, Timmer called for an across-the-board 20%
reduction in head count. He also stipulated that
resources for essential new initiatives would have to
come from within, despite deep cuts in expenses
throughout the company. The meeting broke up to allow
managers from each product division to come to grips
with what they had been presented and to consider how
they would respond. Before this initial session with
Timmer ended, each of the division managers had orally
agreed on targets for reductions in head count and operating costs. In subsequent discussions, those plans
became formal budget agreements between Timmer and
his Centurion managers: Each plan was signed by the
presenting manager to signify his personal commitment

to the terms. Performance would be measured against achievement of the targets and linked to individual bonuses and career opportunities. Personal commitments, binding agreements, and standards for performance would form the basis for the new personal compacts at Philips.

The De Ruwenberg meeting has become part of Philips's company lore. It underscored the urgency of the company's situation and set the stage for the compact-revision process that followed. In the days and weeks thereafter, Timmer maintained a high profile as he spread the message of Operation Centurion and the significance of the new personal compacts. Regular budget reviews gave him opportunities to reinforce his message about personal commitments to current goals. Ongoing meetings with Philips's top 100 managers were the forum for discussing long-term plans.

But Timmer knew that he could not accomplish his goals unless managers and subordinates throughout the company were also committed to change. Employees' concerns about this corporate initiative had to be addressed. Therefore, as the objectives for Operation Centurion came into focus at senior levels, plans to extend its reach emerged. Senior managers negotiated Centurion contracts with their business unit directors, and that group then took the initiative to the product-group and country-management teams. At workshops and training programs, employees at all levels talked about the consequences and objectives of change. Timmer reached out via company "town meetings" to answer questions and talk about the future. His approach made people feel included, and his direct style encouraged them to support him. It soon became clear that employees were listening and the company was changing.

By the end of 1991, the workforce had been cut by 22%—68,000 people. Those who didn't meet the terms of their contracts were gone, including Timmer's successor in the consumer electronics division. Even at the top, the culture of patronage, social networking, and lifetime employment in exchange for loyalty became things of the past. When no one inside qualified, Timmer hired top managers from outside. As a result, by mid-1994, only 4 members of the original senior-management committee remained, and only 5 of the 14 were Dutch. A company survey in 1994 confirmed that employees had responded favorably to the changes and the new atmosphere: Morale and feelings of empowerment had soared. After fluctuating during the early nineties, Philips's financial performance recovered strongly in 1993 and 1994; operating income rose from (4.3%) of sales in 1990 to 6.2% in 1994 and the share price moved from 20.30 guilders to 51.40 guilders.

Of course, not every case is like Philips's. You do not need a crisis to revise personal compacts and get greater commitment. The contrasting example of Eisai, a Japanese health-care company, shows how far the understanding of personal compacts can take you when change is proactive.

CREATING THE CONTEXT FOR CHANGE AT EISAI

A small, family-owned company, Eisai was one of the original manufacturers of vitamin E, and it maintained a strong research commitment to natural pharmaceuticals. Over the years, it developed drugs for the treatment of cardiovascular, respiratory, and neurological diseases; by the end of the 1980s, such drugs comprised 60% of the company's sales. The company experienced steady, modest growth during that decade, and in 1989 sales reached 197 billion yen and profits approached 13 billion yen. But there were signs of potential trouble ahead. Eisai was spending a hefty 13% of sales on R&D—compared with an average of 8.5% in other companies—and between 1982 and 1991, only 12 of the company's 295 patent applications in Japan had been approved by regulatory authorities. Although it was the sixth-largest Japanese pharmaceutical company, Eisai was a relatively small player in an industry in which global competition was increasing while growth in the domestic market was slowing down.

In 1988, Haruo Naito took over as CEO and president from his father. Before that, he had chaired Eisai's five-year strategic planning committee. During that time, he had become convinced that the company's focus on the discovery and manufacture of pharmaceuticals was not sustainable for long-term growth against large, global competitors. In the absence of either a real or a perceived crisis, however, and in the face of deeply felt cultural traditions, changing direction at Eisai would require unusual leadership.

In the tradition of Japanese family companies, Eisai had few formal rules of employment. Among the 4,000 employees, lifelong employment was the norm and career advancement and authority were based on seniority. Groups made decisions because failure by an individual would mean loss of face. And employees were not encouraged to step outside established roles to take on assignments beyond the scope and structure of the existing organization. Individuals were loyal both to their managers and to group norms, so they did not seek personal recognition or accomplishment. And because other

Japanese companies operated in similar ways, there was no external competitive pressure to be different. To accomplish strategic transformation, Naito would have to create a compelling context for change and an inducement for employees to try something new—without disrupting the entire organization.

Several years after becoming CEO, Naito formulated a radical new vision for Eisai that he called Human Health Care (HHC). It extended the company's focus from manufacturing drug treatments for specific illnesses to improving the overall quality of life, especially for elderly sick people. To accomplish that mission, Eisai would have to develop a wide array of new products and services. And that, in turn, would require broad employee involvement and commitment. Although Naito did not explicitly characterize Eisai employees' commitments as personal compacts, he clearly understood that individuals would have to accept new terms and performance standards that he could not simply mandate. He had to encourage entrepreneurial and innovative activity and create an environment in which such efforts would be accepted and rewarded. Indeed, for his vision of HHC to become reality, Naito knew that employees themselves would ultimately have to take the lead in designing the formal terms of their personal compacts.

In 1989, Naito announced his new strategic vision and initiated a training program for 103 "innovation managers" who were to become the agents for change in the company. The training program consisted of seminars on trends in health care and concepts of organizational change. It also gave employees a firsthand look at patient-care practices by having them spend several days in both traditional and nontraditional health-care facilities where they performed actual nursing activities. At the end of the program, Naito charged the innovation managers with turning the insights from their experiences into proposals for new products and services. Each proposal was brought before Naito and Eisai's executive management to gain high-level corporate support and, as important to Naito, to secure individual managers' public commitment to the achievement of their HHC projects' goals.

This training program and the subsequent HHC product-development efforts set the stage for the creation of a dramatically different set of personal compacts at Eisai. The innovation managers operated outside both the normal organizational structure and the company's traditional cultural boundaries. They designed new products and programs, put together multidisciplinary teams to develop their ideas, and drew new participants of their own choice into the change initiative. They reported to Naito, and he personally evaluated their performance and the contribution of individual projects to the HHC vision. As a result, junior people had a chance to break out of the seniority system and to shape the development of the company's new strategy as well as the terms of their own personal compacts. These were opportunities previously unheard of in Eisai or in other Japanese pharmaceutical companies.

The visibility and senior-management support for the first projects generated widespread enthusiasm for participating in the new movement at Eisai. The cross-functional teams established employee ownership of the HHC vision, which rapidly took on a life of its own. Soon there were proposals for 130 additional HHC projects involving 900 people, and by the end of 1993, 73 projects were under way. New services offered by the company included a 24-hour telephone line to assist people taking

Eisai medications. Another brought consumers and medical professionals together at conferences to discuss health-care needs. New attention to consumer preferences led to improvements in the packaging and delivery of medications.

Although personal compacts at Eisai are still dominated by traditional cultural norms, Naito's ability to lead his employees through a process in which they examined and revised the old terms enabled them to accomplish major strategic change. The effects of the new strategy are visible in Eisai's product mix. By the end of 1993, the company had moved from sixth to fifth place in the Japanese domestic pharmaceutical industry, and today Eisai's customers and competitors view the company as a leader in health care.

Culture and Personal Compacts

The extent to which personal compacts are written or oral varies with the organization's culture and, in many cases, the company's home country. In general, the more homogeneous the culture, the more implicit the formal dimension of personal compacts is likely to be. The same is true along psychological and social dimensions in homogeneous environments, because employers and employees share similar perspectives and expectations. For example, in Japan and continental Europe, the legal systems for settling disputes are based on a civil code documented in statutes. Those systems carry over to the underlying principles in legal contracts and to the assumptions that support employer-employee relationships. Indeed, when a compact is laid out too explicitly in Japan, it is taken as an affront and a sign that one party doesn't understand how things work.

By contrast, in countries like the United States, personal compacts tend to be supported by formal systems to ensure objectivity in the standards for performance evaluation. And more structure exists to support employee-employer relations, both in the form of company policies and procedures and in the role that human resource departments play. Similarly, as companies become more truly multinational, the importance of making the terms of personal compacts explicit increases, as does the requirement to support them formally. In my experience, this is true whether companies are implementing change to meet the needs of a culturally diverse workforce or to respond to market opportunities and threats.

Regardless of the cultural context, unless the revision of personal compacts is treated as integral to the change process, companies will not accomplish their goals. In one way or another, leaders must take charge of the process and address each dimension. Jan Timmer and Haruo Naito revised their employees' personal compacts using different approaches and for different reasons. But each drove successful corporate change by redefining his employees' commitment to new goals in terms that everyone could understand and act on. Without such leadership, employees will remain skeptical of the vision for change and distrustful of management, and management will likewise be frustrated and stymied by employees' resistance.

Originally published in May–June 1996
Reprint 96310

Conquering a
Culture of Indecision

RAM CHARAN

Executive Summary

THE SINGLE GREATEST CAUSE of corporate under-performance is the failure to execute. Author Ram Charan, drawing on a quarter century of observing organizational behavior, perceives that such failures of execution share a family resemblance: a misfire in the personal interactions that are supposed to produce results.

Faulty interactions rarely occur in isolation, Charan says. Far more often, they're typical of the way large and small decisions are made or not made throughout the organization. The inability to take decisive action is rooted in a company's culture.

But, Charan notes, leaders create a culture of indecisiveness, and leaders can break it. Breaking it requires them to take three actions. First, they must engender intellectual honesty in the connections between people. Second, they must see to it that the organization's "social operating mechanisms"—the meetings, reviews, and other situations through which people in the corporation do business—have honest dialogue at their cores. And third, leaders must ensure that feedback and follow-through are used to reward high achievers, coach those who are struggling, and discourage those whose behaviors are blocking the organization's progress.

By taking these three approaches and using every encounter as an opportunity to model open and honest dialogue, a leader can set the tone for an organization, moving it from paralysis to action.

DOES THIS SOUND FAMILIAR? You're sitting in the quarterly business review as a colleague plows through a two-inch-thick proposal for a big investment in a new product. When he finishes, the room falls quiet. People look left, right, or down, waiting for someone else to open the discussion. No one wants to comment—at least not until the boss shows which way he's leaning.

Finally, the CEO breaks the loud silence. He asks a few mildly skeptical questions to show he's done his due diligence. But it's clear that he has made up his mind to back the project. Before long, the other meeting attendees are chiming in dutifully, careful to keep their comments positive. Judging from the remarks, it appears that everyone in the room supports the project.

But appearances can be deceiving. The head of a related division worries that the new product will take resources away from his operation. The vice president of manufacturing thinks that the first-year sales forecasts are wildly optimistic and will leave him with a warehouse full of unsold goods. Others in the room are lukewarm because they don't see how they stand to gain from the project. But they keep their reservations to themselves, and the meeting breaks up inconclusively. Over the next few months, the project is slowly strangled to death in a series of strategy, budget, and operational reviews. It's not clear who's responsible for the killing, but it's plain that the true sentiment in the room was the opposite of the apparent consensus.

In my career as an adviser to large organizations and their leaders, I have witnessed many occasions even at the highest levels when silent lies and a lack of closure lead to false decisions. They are "false" because they eventually get undone by unspoken factors and inaction. And after a quarter century of firsthand observations, I have concluded that these instances of indecision share a family resemblance—a misfire in the personal interactions that are supposed to produce results. The people charged with reaching a decision and acting on it fail to connect and engage with one another. Intimidated by the group dynamics of hierarchy and constrained by formality and lack of trust, they speak their lines woodenly and without conviction. Lacking emotional commitment, the people who must carry out the plan don't act decisively.

These faulty interactions rarely occur in isolation. Far more often, they're typical of the way large and small decisions are made—or not made—throughout a company. The inability to take decisive action is rooted in the corporate culture and seems to employees to be impervious to change.

The key word here is "seems," because, in fact, leaders create a culture of indecisiveness, and leaders can break it. The primary instrument at their disposal is the human interactions—the dialogues—through which assumptions are challenged or go unchallenged, information is shared or not shared, disagreements are brought to the surface or papered over. Dialogue is the basic unit of work in an organization. The quality of the dialogue determines how people gather and process information, how they make decisions, and how they feel about one another and about the outcome of these decisions. Dialogue can lead to new ideas and speed as a competitive advantage. It is the single-most important factor underlying the productivity and growth of the knowledge worker. Indeed, the tone and content of dialogue shapes people's behaviors and beliefs—that is, the corporate culture—faster and more permanently than any reward system, structural change, or vision statement I've seen.

Breaking a culture of indecision requires a leader who can engender intellectual honesty and trust in the connections between people. By using each encounter with his or her employees as an opportunity to model open, honest, and decisive dialogue, the leader sets the tone for the entire organization.

But setting the tone is only the first step. To transform a culture of indecision, leaders must also see to it that the organization's "social operating mechanisms"— that is, the executive committee meetings, budget and strategy reviews, and other situations through which the people of a corporation do business—have honest dialogue at their center. These mechanisms set the stage. Tightly linked and consistently practiced, they establish clear lines of accountability for reaching decisions and executing them.

Follow-through and feedback are the final steps in creating a decisive culture. Successful leaders use follow-through and honest feedback to reward high achievers, coach those who are struggling, and redirect the behaviors of those blocking the organization's progress.

In sum, leaders can create a culture of decisive behavior through attention to their own dialogue, the careful design of social operating mechanisms, and appropriate follow-through and feedback.

It All Begins with Dialogue

Studies of successful companies often focus on their products, business models, or operational strengths: Microsoft's world-conquering Windows operating system, Dell's mass customization, Wal-Mart's logistical prowess. Yet products and operational strengths aren't what really set the most successful organizations apart—they can all be rented or imitated. What can't be easily duplicated are the decisive dialogues and robust operating mechanisms and their links to feedback and follow-through. These factors constitute an organization's most enduring competitive advantage, and they are heavily dependent on the character of dialogue that a leader exhibits and thereby influences throughout the organization.

Decisive dialogue is easier to recognize than to define. It encourages incisiveness and creativity and brings coherence to seemingly fragmented and unrelated ideas. It allows tensions to surface and then resolves them by fully airing every relevant viewpoint. Because such dialogue is a process of intellectual inquiry rather than of advocacy, a search for truth rather than a contest, people feel emotionally committed to the outcome. The outcome seems "right" because people have helped shape it. They are energized and ready to act.

Not long ago, I observed the power of a leader's dialogue to shape a company's culture. The setting was the headquarters of a major U.S. multinational. The head of

one of the company's largest business units was making
a strategy presentation to the CEO and a few of his
senior lieutenants. Sounding confident, almost cocky,
the unit head laid out his strategy for taking his division
from number three in Europe to number one. It was an
ambitious plan that hinged on making rapid, sizable
market-share gains in Germany, where the company's
main competitor was locally based and four times his
division's size. The CEO commended his unit head for
the inspiring and visionary presentation, then initiated a
dialogue to test whether the plan was realistic. "Just how
are you going to make these gains?" he wondered aloud.
"What other alternatives have you considered? What
customers do you plan to acquire?" The unit manager
hadn't thought that far ahead. "How have you defined
the customers' needs in new and unique ways? How
many salespeople do you have?" the CEO asked.

"Ten," answered the unit head.

"How many does your main competitor have?"

"Two hundred," came the sheepish reply.

The boss continued to press: "Who runs Germany for
us? Wasn't he in another division up until about three
months ago?"

Had the exchange stopped there, the CEO would have
only humiliated and discouraged this unit head and sent a
message to others in attendance that the risks of thinking
big were unacceptably high. But the CEO wasn't inter-
ested in killing the strategy and demoralizing the business unit team. Coaching through questioning, he wanted
to inject some realism into the dialogue. Speaking bluntly,
but not angrily or unkindly, he told the unit manager that
he would need more than bravado to take on a formidable
German competitor on its home turf. Instead of making a
frontal assault, the CEO suggested, why not look for the

competition's weak spots and win on speed of execution? Where are the gaps in your competitor's product line? Can you innovate something that can fill those gaps? What customers are the most likely buyers of such a product? Why not zero in on them? Instead of aiming for overall market-share gains, try resegmenting the market. Suddenly, what had appeared to be a dead end opened into new insights, and by the end of the meeting, it was decided that the manager would rethink the strategy and return in 90 days with a more realistic alternative. A key player whose strategy proposal had been flatly rejected left the room feeling energized, challenged, and more sharply focused on the task at hand.

Think about what happened here. Although it might not have been obvious at first, the CEO was not trying to assert his authority or diminish the executive. He simply wanted to ensure that the competitive realities were not glossed over and to coach those in attendance on both business acumen and organizational capability as well as on the fine art of asking the right questions. He was challenging the proposed strategy not for personal reasons but for business reasons.

The dialogue affected people's attitudes and behavior in subtle and not so subtle ways: they walked away knowing that they should look for opportunities in unconventional ways and be prepared to answer the inevitable tough questions. They also knew that the CEO was on their side. They became more convinced that growth was possible and that action was necessary. And something else happened: they began to adopt the CEO's tone in subsequent meetings. When, for example, the head of the German unit met with his senior staff to brief them on the new approach to the German market, the questions he fired at his sales chief and product development head were pointed, precise, and aimed directly at putting the new strategy into action. He had picked up on his boss's style of relating to others as well as his way of eliciting, sifting, and analyzing information. The entire unit grew more determined and energized.

The chief executive didn't leave the matter there, though. He followed up with a one-page, handwritten letter to the unit head stating the essence of the dialogue and the actions to be executed. And in 90 days, they met again to discuss the revised strategy. (For more on fostering decisive dialogue, see "Dialogue Killers" at the end of this article.)

How Dialogue Becomes Action

The setting in which dialogue occurs is as important as the dialogue itself. The social operating mechanisms of decisive corporate cultures feature behaviors marked by four characteristics: openness, candor, informality, and closure. Openness means that the outcome is not predetermined. There's an honest search for alternatives and new discoveries. Questions like "What are we missing?" draw people in and signal the leader's willingness to hear all sides. Leaders create an atmosphere of safety that permits spirited discussion, group learning, and trust.

Candor is slightly different. It's a willingness to speak the unspeakable, to expose unfulfilled commitments, to air the conflicts that undermine apparent consensus. Candor means that people express their real opinions, not what they think team players are supposed to say. Candor helps wipe out the silent lies and pocket vetoes that occur when people agree to things they have no intention of acting on. It prevents the kind of unnecessary rework and revisiting of decisions that saps productivity.

Formality suppresses candor; informality encourages it. When presentations and comments are stiff and prepackaged, they signal that the whole meeting has been carefully scripted and orchestrated. Informality has the opposite effect. It reduces defensiveness. People feel more comfortable asking questions and reacting honestly, and the spontaneity is energizing.

If informality loosens the atmosphere, closure imposes discipline. Closure means that at the end of the meeting, people know exactly what they are expected to do. Closure produces decisiveness by assigning accountability and deadlines to people in an open forum. It tests a leader's inner strength and intellectual resources. Lack of closure, coupled with a lack of sanctions, is the primary reason for a culture of indecision.

A robust social operating mechanism consistently includes these four characteristics. Such a mechanism has the right people participating in it, and it occurs with the right frequency.

When Dick Brown arrived at Electronic Data Systems (EDS) in early 1999, he resolved to create a culture that did more than pay lip service to the ideals of collaboration, openness, and decisiveness. He had a big job ahead of him. EDS was known for its bright, aggressive people, but employees had a reputation for competing against one another at least as often as they pulled together. The organization was marked by a culture of lone heroes. Individual operating units had little or no incentive for sharing information or cooperating with one another to win business. There were few sanctions for "lone" behaviors and for failure to meet performance goals. And indecision was rife. As one company veteran puts it, "Meetings, meetings, and more meetings. People couldn't make decisions, wouldn't make decisions. They didn't have to. No accountability." EDS was losing business. Revenue was flat, earnings were on the decline, and the price of the company's stock was down sharply.

A central tenet of Brown's management philosophy is that "leaders get the behavior they tolerate." Shortly after he arrived at EDS, he installed six social operating mechanisms within one year that signaled he would not put up with the old culture of rampant individualism and information hoarding. One mechanism was the "performance call," as it is known around the company. Once a month, the top 100 or so EDS executives worldwide take part in a conference call where the past month's numbers and critical activities are reviewed in detail. Transparency and simultaneous information are the rules; information hoarding is no longer possible. Everyone knows who is on target for the year, who is ahead of projections, and who is behind. Those who are behind must explain the shortfall—and how they plan to get back on track. It's not enough for a manager to say she's assessing, reviewing, or analyzing a problem. Those aren't the words of someone who is acting, Brown says. Those are the words of someone getting ready to act. To use them in front of Brown is to invite two questions in response: When you've finished your analysis, what are you going to do? And how soon are you going to do it? The only way that Brown's people can answer those questions satisfactorily is to make a decision and execute it.

The performance calls are also a mechanism for airing and resolving the conflicts inevitable in a large organization, particularly when it comes to cross-selling in order to accelerate revenue growth. Two units may be pursuing the same customer, for example, or a customer serviced by one unit may be acquired by a customer serviced by another. Which unit should lead the pursuit? Which unit should service the merged entity? It's vitally important to resolve these questions. Letting them fester doesn't just drain emotional energy, it shrinks the organization's capacity to act decisively. Lack of speed becomes a competitive disadvantage.

Brown encourages people to bring these conflicts to the surface, both because he views them as a sign of organizational health and because they provide an opportunity to demonstrate the style of dialogue he advocates. He tries to create a safe environment for disagreement by reminding employees that the conflict isn't personal. Conflict in any global organization is built in. And, Brown believes, it's essential if everyone is going to think in terms of the entire organization, not just one little corner of it. Instead of seeking the solution favorable to their unit, they'll look for the solution that's best for EDS and its shareholders. It sounds simple, even obvious. But in an organization once characterized by lone heroes and self-interest, highly visible exercises in conflict resolution remind people to align their interests with the company as a whole. It's not enough to state the message once and assume it will sink in. Behavior is changed through repetition. Stressing the message over and over in social operating mechanisms like the monthly performance calls—and rewarding or sanctioning people based on their adherence to it—is one of Brown's most powerful tools for producing the behavioral changes that usher in genuine cultural change.

Of course, no leader can or should attend every meeting, resolve every conflict, or make every decision. But by designing social operating mechanisms that promote free-flowing yet productive dialogue, leaders strongly influence how others perform these tasks. Indeed, it is through these mechanisms that the work of shaping a decisive culture gets done.

Another corporation that employs social operating mechanisms to create a decisive culture is multinational pharmaceutical giant Pharmacia. The company's approach illustrates a point I stress repeatedly to my clients: structure divides; social operating mechanisms integrate. I hasten to add that structure is essential. If an organization didn't divide tasks, functions, and responsibilities, it would never get anything done. But social operating mechanisms are required to direct the various activities contained within a structure toward an objective. Well-designed mechanisms perform this integrating function. But no matter how well designed, the mechanisms also need decisive dialogue to work properly.

Two years after its 1995 merger with Upjohn, Pharmacia's CEO Fred Hassan set out to create an entirely new culture for the combined entity. The organization he envisioned would be collaborative, customer focused, and speedy. It would meld the disparate talents of a global enterprise to develop market-leading drugs—and do so faster than the competition. The primary mechanism for fostering collaboration: leaders from several units and functions would engage in frequent, constructive dialogue.

The company's race to develop a new generation of antibiotics to treat drug-resistant infections afforded Pharmacia's management an opportunity to test the success of its culture-building efforts. Dr. Göran Endo, the chief of research and development, and Carrie Cox, the head of global business management, jointly created a social operating mechanism comprising some of the company's leading scientists, clinicians, and marketers. Just getting the three functions together regularly was a bold step.

Typically, drug development proceeds by a series of hand-offs. One group of scientists does the basic work of drug discovery, then hands off its results to a second group, which steers the drug through a year or more of clinical trials. If and when it receives the Food and Drug Administration's stamp of approval, it's handed off to the marketing people, who devise a marketing plan. Only then is the drug handed off to the sales department, which pitches it to doctors and hospitals. By supplanting this daisy-chain approach with one that made scientists, clinicians, and marketers jointly responsible for the entire flow of development and marketing, the two leaders aimed to develop a drug that better met the needs of patients, had higher revenue potential, and gained speed as a competitive advantage. And they wanted to create a template for future collaborative efforts.

The company's reward system reinforced this collaborative model by explicitly linking compensation to the actions of the group. Every member's compensation would be based on the time to bring the drug to market, the time for the drug to reach peak profitable share, and total sales. The system gave group members a strong incentive to talk openly with one another and to share information freely. But the creative spark was missing. The first few times the drug development group met, it focused almost exclusively on their differences, which were considerable. Without trafficking in clichés, it is safe to say that scientists, clinicians, and marketers tend to have different ways of speaking, thinking, and relating. And each tended to defend what it viewed as its interests rather than the interests of shareholders and customers. It was at this point that Endo and Cox took charge of the dialogue, reminding the group that it was important to play well with others but, even more important, to produce a drug that met patients' needs and to beat the competition.

Acting together, the two leaders channeled conversation into productive dialogue focused on a common task. They shared what they knew about developing and marketing pharmaceuticals and demonstrated how scientists could learn to think a little like marketers, and marketers a little like scientists. They tackled the emotional challenge of resolving conflicts in the open in order to demonstrate how to disagree, sometimes strongly, without animosity and without losing sight of their common purpose.

Indeed, consider how one dialogue helped the group make a decision that turned a promising drug into a success story. To simplify the research and testing process, the group's scientists had begun to search for an antibiotic that would be effective against a limited number of infections and would be used only as "salvage therapy" in acute cases, when conventional antibiotic therapies had failed. But intensive dialogue with the marketers yielded the information that doctors were receptive to a drug that would work against a wide spectrum of infections. They wanted a drug that could treat acute infections completely by starting treatment earlier in the course of the disease, either in large doses through an intravenous drip or in smaller doses with a pill. The scientists shifted their focus, and the result was Zyvox, one of the major pharmaceutical success stories of recent years. It has become the poster drug in Pharmacia's campaign for a culture characterized by cross-functional collaboration and speedy execution. Through dialogue, the group created a product that neither the scientists, clinicians, nor marketers acting by themselves could have envisioned or executed. And the mechanism that created this open dialogue is now standard practice at Pharmacia.

Follow-Through and Feedback

Follow-through is in the DNA of decisive cultures and takes place either in person, on the telephone, or in the routine conduct of a social operating mechanism. Lack of follow-through destroys the discipline of execution and encourages indecision.

A culture of indecision changes when groups of people are compelled to always be direct. And few mechanisms encourage directness more effectively than performance and compensation reviews, especially if they are explicitly linked to social operating mechanisms. Yet all too often, the performance review process is as ritualized and empty as the business meeting I described at the beginning of this article. Both the employee and his manager want to get the thing over with as quickly as possible. Check the appropriate box, keep up the good work, here's your raise, and let's be sure to do this again next year. Sorry—gotta run. There's no genuine conversation, no feedback, and worst of all, no chance for the employee to learn the sometimes painful truths that will help her grow and develop. Great compensation systems die for lack of candid dialogue and leaders' emotional fortitude.

At EDS, Dick Brown has devised an evaluation and review process that virtually forces managers to engage in candid dialogue with their subordinates. Everyone at the company is ranked in quintiles and rewarded according to how well they perform compared with their peers. It has proved to be one of the most controversial features of Dick Brown's leadership—some employees view it as a

Darwinian means of dividing winners from losers and pitting colleagues against one another.

That isn't the objective of the ranking system, Brown insists. He views the ranking process as the most effective way to reward the company's best performers and show laggards where they need to improve. But the system needs the right sort of dialogue to make it work as intended and serve its purpose of growing the talent pool. Leaders must give honest feedback to their direct reports, especially to those who find themselves at the bottom of the rankings.

Brown recalls one encounter he had shortly after the first set of rankings was issued. An employee who had considered himself one of EDS's best performers was shocked to find himself closer to the bottom of the roster than the top. "How could this be?" the employee asked. "I performed as well this year as I did last year, and last year my boss gave me a stellar review." Brown replied that he could think of two possible explanations. The first was that the employee wasn't as good at his job as he thought he was. The second possibility was that even if the employee was doing as good a job as he did the previous year, his peers were doing better. "If you're staying the same," Brown concluded, "you're falling behind."

That exchange revealed the possibility—the likelihood, even—that the employee's immediate superior had given him a less-than-honest review the year before rather than tackle the unpleasant task of telling him where he was coming up short. Brown understands why a manager might be tempted to duck such a painful conversation. Delivering negative feedback tests the strength of a leader. But critical feedback is part of what Brown calls "the heavy lifting of leadership." Avoiding it, he says, "sentences the organization to mediocrity." What's more, by failing to provide honest feedback, leaders cheat their people by depriving them of the information they need to improve.

Feedback should be many things—candid; constructive; relentlessly focused on behavioral performance, accountability, and execution. One thing it shouldn't be is surprising. "A leader should be constructing his appraisal all year long," Brown says, "and giving his appraisal all year long. You have 20, 30, 60 opportunities a year to share your observations. Don't let those opportunities pass. If, at the end of the year, someone is truly surprised by what you have to say, that's a failure of leadership."

ULTIMATELY, changing a culture of indecision is a matter of leadership. It's a matter of asking hard questions: How robust and effective are our social operating mechanisms? How well are they linked? Do they have the right people and the right frequency? Do they have a rhythm and operate consistently? Is follow-through built in? Are rewards and sanctions linked to the outcomes of the decisive dialogue? Most important, how productive is the dialogue within these mechanisms? Is our dialogue marked by openness, candor, informality, and closure?

Transforming a culture of indecision is an enormous and demanding task. It takes all the listening skills, business acumen, and operational experience that a corporate leader can summon. But just as important, the job demands emotional fortitude, follow-through, and inner strength. Asking the right questions, identifying and resolving conflicts, providing candid, constructive feedback, and differentiating people with sanctions and rewards is never easy. Frequently, it's downright unpleasant. No wonder many senior executives avoid the task. In the short term, they spare themselves considerable emotional wear and tear. But their evasion sets the tone for an organization that can't share intelligence, make decisions, or face conflicts, much less resolve them. Those who evade miss the very point of effective leadership. Leaders with the strength to insist on honest dialogue and follow-through will be rewarded not only with a decisive organization but also with a workforce that is energized, empowered, and engaged.

Dialogue Killers

IS THE DIALOGUE in your meetings an energy drain? If it doesn't energize people and focus their work, watch for the following:

Dangling Dialogue

Symptom: Confusion prevails. The meeting ends without a clear next step. People create their own self-serving interpretations of the meeting, and no one can be held accountable later when goals aren't met.

Remedy: Give the meeting closure by ensuring that everyone knows who will do what, by when. Do it in writing if necessary, and be specific.

Information Clogs

Symptom: Failure to get all the relevant information into the open. An important fact or opinion comes to light after a decision has been reached, which reopens the decision. This pattern happens repeatedly.

Remedy: Ensure that the right people are in attendance in the first place. When missing information is discovered, disseminate it immediately. Make the expectation for openness and candor explicit by asking, "What's missing?" Use coaching and sanctions to correct information hoarding.

Piecemeal Perspectives

Symptom: People stick to narrow views and self-interests and fail to acknowledge that others have valid interests.

Remedy: Draw people out until you're sure all sides of the issue have been represented. Restate the common purpose repeatedly to keep everyone focused on the big picture. Generate alternatives. Use coaching to show people how their work contributes to the overall mission of the enterprise.

Free for All

Symptom: By failing to direct the flow of the discussion, the leader allows negative behaviors to flourish. "Extortionists" hold the whole group for ransom until others see it their way; "sidetrackers" go off on tangents, recount history by saying "When I did this ten years ago . . . ", or delve into unnecessary detail; "silent liars" do not express their true opinions, or they agree to things they have no intention of doing; and "dividers" create breaches within the group by seeking support for their viewpoint outside the social operating mechanism or have parallel discussions during the meeting.

Remedy: The leader must exercise inner strength by repeatedly signaling which behaviors are acceptable and by sanctioning those who persist in negative behavior. If less severe sanctions fail, the leader must be willing to remove the offending player from the group.

GE's Secret Weapon

KNOWN FOR ITS STATE-OF-THE-ART management practices, General Electric has forged a system of ten tightly linked social operating mechanisms. Vital to GE's success, these mechanisms set goals and priorities for the whole company as well as for its individual business units and track each unit's progress toward those goals. CEO Jack Welch also uses the system to evaluate senior managers within each unit and reward or sanction them according to their performance.

Three of the most widely imitated of these mechanisms are the Corporate Executive Council (CEC), which meets four times a year; the annual leadership and organizational reviews, known as Session C; and the annual strategy reviews, known as S-1 and S-2. Most large organizations have similar mechanisms. GE's, however, are notable for their intensity and duration; tight links to one another; follow-through; and uninhibited candor, closure, and decisiveness.

At the CEC, the company's senior leaders gather for two-and-a-half days of intensive collaboration and information exchange. As these leaders share best practices, assess the external business environment, and identify the company's most promising opportunities and most pressing problems, Welch has a chance to coach managers and observe their styles of working, thinking, and collaborating. Among the ten initiatives to emerge from these meetings in the past 14 years are GE's six sigma quality-improvement drive and its companywide e-commerce effort. These sessions aren't for the fainthearted—at times, the debates can resemble verbal combat. But by the time the CEC breaks up, everyone in attendance knows both what the corporate priorities are and what's expected of him or her.

At Session C meetings, Welch and GE's senior vice president for human resources, Bill Conaty, meet with the head of each business unit as well as his or her top HR executive to discuss leadership and organizational issues. In these intense 12- to 14-hour sessions, the attendees review the unit's prospective talent pool and its organizational priorities. Who needs to be promoted, rewarded, and developed? How? Who isn't making the grade? Candor is mandatory, and so is execution. The dialogue goes back and forth and links with the strategy of the business unit. Welch follows up each session with a handwritten note reviewing the substance of the dialogue and action items. Through this mechanism, picking and evaluating people has become a core competence at GE. No wonder GE is known as "CEO University."

The unit head's progress in implementing that action plan is among the items on the agenda at the S-1 meeting, held about two months after Session C. Welch, his chief financial officer, and members of the office of the CEO meet individually with each unit head and his or her team to discuss strategy for the next three years. The strategy, which must incorporate the companywide themes and initiatives that emerged from the CEC meetings, is subjected to intensive scrutiny and reality testing by Welch and the senior staff. The dialogue in the sessions is informal, open, decisive, and full of valuable coaching from Welch on both business and human resources issues. As in Session C, the dialogue about strategy links with people and organizational issues. Again, Welch follows up with a handwritten note in which he sets out what he expects of the unit head as a result of the dialogue.

S-2 meetings, normally held in November, follow a similar agenda to the S-1 meeting, except that they are focused on a shorter time horizon, usually 12 to 15 months. Here, operational priorities and resource allocations are linked.

Taken together, the meetings link feedback, decision making, and assessment of the organization's capabilities and key people. The mechanism explicitly ties the goals and performance of each unit to the overall strategy of the corporation and places a premium on the development of the next generation of leaders. The process is unrelenting in its demand for managerial accountability. At the same time, Welch takes the opportunity to engage in follow-through and feedback that is candid, on point, and focused on decisiveness and execution. This operating system may be GE's most enduring competitive advantage.

Originally published in April 2001
Reprint R0104D

Change Through Persuasion

DAVID A. GARVIN AND

MICHAEL A. ROBERTO

Executive Summary

FACED WITH THE NEED for a massive change, most managers respond predictably. They revamp the organization's strategy, shift around staff, and root out inefficiencies. They then wait patiently for performance to improve—only to be bitterly disappointed because they've failed to adequately prepare employees for the change. In this article, the authors contend that to make change stick, leaders must conduct an effective persuasion campaign—one that begins weeks or months before the turnaround plan is set in concrete.

Like a political campaign, a persuasion campaign is largely one of differentiation from the past. Turnaround leaders must convince people that the organization is truly on its deathbed—or, at the very least, that radical changes are required if the organization is to survive and thrive. (This is a particularly difficult challenge when years of persistent problems have been accompanied by few changes in the status quo.) And they must demonstrate through word and deed that they are the right leaders with the right plan.

Accomplishing all this calls for a four-part communications strategy. Prior to announcing a turnaround plan, leaders need to set the stage for employees' acceptance of it. At the time of delivery, they must present a framework through which employees can interpret information and messages about the plan. As time passes, they must manage the mood so that employees' emotional states support implementation and follow-through. And at critical intervals, they must provide reinforcement to ensure that the desired changes take hold and that there's no backsliding.

Using the example of the dramatic turnaround at Boston's Beth Israel Deaconess Medical Center, the authors elucidate the inner workings of a successful change effort.

Faced with the need for massive change, most managers respond predictably. They revamp the organization's strategy, then round up the usual set of suspects—people, pay, and processes—shifting around staff, realigning incentives, and rooting out inefficiencies. They then wait patiently for performance to improve, only to be bitterly disappointed. For some reason, the right things still don't happen.

Why is change so hard? First of all, most people are reluctant to alter their habits. What worked in the past is good enough; in the absence of a dire threat, employees will keep doing what they've always done. And when an organization has had a succession of leaders, resistance to change is even stronger. A legacy of disappointment and distrust creates an environment in which employees automatically condemn the next turnaround champion to failure, assuming that he or she is "just like all the others." Calls for sacrifice and self-discipline are met with cynicism, skepticism, and knee-jerk resistance.

Our research into organizational transformation has involved settings as diverse as multinational corporations, government agencies, nonprofits, and high-performing teams like mountaineering expeditions and firefighting crews. We've found that for change to stick, leaders must design and run an effective persuasion campaign—one that begins weeks or months before the actual turnaround plan is set in concrete. Managers must perform significant work up front to ensure that employees will actually listen to tough messages, question old assumptions, and consider new ways of working. This means taking a series of deliberate but subtle steps to recast employees' prevailing views and create a new context for action. Such a shaping process must be actively managed during the first few months of a turnaround, when uncertainty is high and setbacks are inevitable. Otherwise, there is little hope for sustained improvement.

Like a political campaign, a persuasion campaign is largely one of differentiation from the past. To the typical change-averse employee, all restructuring plans look alike. The trick for turnaround leaders is to show employees precisely how their plans differ from their predecessors'. They must convince people that the organization is truly on its deathbed—or, at the very least, that radical changes are required if it is to survive and thrive. (This is a particularly difficult challenge when years of persistent problems have been accompanied by few changes in the status quo.) Turnaround leaders must also gain trust by demonstrating through word and deed that they are the right leaders for the job and must convince employees that theirs is the correct plan for moving forward.

Accomplishing all this calls for a four-part communications strategy. Prior to announcing a policy or issuing a set of instructions, leaders need to set the stage for acceptance. At the time of delivery, they must create the frame through which information and messages are interpreted. As time passes, they must manage the mood so that employees' emotional states support implementation and follow-through. And at critical intervals, they must provide reinforcement to ensure that the desired changes take hold without backsliding. See the exhibit "The Four Phases of a Persuasion Campaign" for a graphical reproduction.

In this article, we describe this process in more detail, drawing on the example of the turnaround of Beth Israel Deaconess Medical Center (BIDMC) in Boston. Paul Levy, who became CEO in early 2002, managed to bring the failing hospital back from the brink of ruin. We had ringside seats during the first six months of the turnaround. Levy agreed to hold videotaped interviews with us every two to four weeks during that period as we prepared a case study describing his efforts. He also gave us access to his daily calendar, as well as to assorted e-mail correspondence and internal memorandums and reports. From this wealth of data, we were able to track the change process as it unfolded, without the usual biases and distortions that come from 20/20 hindsight. The story of how Levy tilled the soil for change provides lessons for any CEO in a turnaround situation.

The Four Phases of a Persuasion Campaign

A typical turnaround process consists of two stark phases: plan development, followed by an implementation that may or may not be welcomed by the organization. For the turnaround plan to be widely accepted and adopted, however, the CEO must develop a separate persuasion campaign, the goal of which is to create a continuously receptive environment for change. The campaign begins well before the CEO's first day on the job—or, if the CEO is long established, well before formal development work begins—and continues long after the final plan is announced.

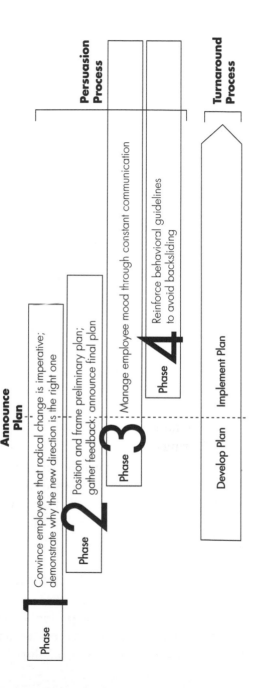

Setting the Stage

Paul Levy was an unlikely candidate to run BIDMC. He was not a doctor and had never managed a hospital, though he had previously served as the executive dean for administration at Harvard Medical School. His claim to fame was his role as the architect of the Boston Harbor Cleanup, a multibillion-dollar pollution-control project that he had led several years earlier. (Based on this experience, Levy identified a common yet insidiously destructive organizational dynamic that causes dedicated teams to operate in counterproductive ways, which he described in "The Nut Island Effect: When Good Teams Go Wrong," HBR March 2001.) Six years after completing the Boston Harbor project, Levy approached the BIDMC board and applied for the job of cleaning up the troubled hospital.

Despite his lack of hospital management experience, Levy was appealing to the board. The Boston Harbor Cleanup was a difficult, highly visible change effort that required deft political and managerial skills. Levy had stood firm in the face of tough negotiations and often-heated public resistance and had instilled accountability in city and state agencies. He was also a known quantity to the board, having served on a BIDMC steering committee formed by the board chairman in 2001.

Levy saw the prospective job as one of public service. BIDMC was the product of a difficult 1996 merger between two hospitals—Beth Israel and Deaconess— each of which had distinguished reputations, several best-in-the-world departments and specializations, and deeply devoted staffs. The problems began after the merger. A misguided focus on clinical practice rather than backroom integration, a failure to cut costs, and the

repeated inability to execute plans and adapt to changing conditions in the health-care marketplace all con-
tributed to BIDMC's dismal performance.

By the time the board settled on Levy, affairs at
BIDMC had reached the nadir. The hospital was losing
$50 million a year. Relations between the administration
and medical staff were strained, as were those between
management and the board of directors. Employees felt
demoralized, having witnessed the rapid decline in their
institution's once-legendary status and the disappoint-
ing failure of its past leaders. A critical study was conducted by the Hunter Group, a leading health-care consulting firm. The report, detailing the dire conditions at
the hospital and the changes needed to turn things
around, had been completed but not yet released. Meanwhile, the state attorney general, who was responsible for
overseeing charitable trusts, had put pressure on the
board to sell the failing BIDMC to a for-profit institution.

Like many CEOs recruited to fix a difficult situation,
Levy's first task was to gain a mandate for the changes
ahead. He also recognized that crucial negotiations
were best conducted before he took the job, when his
leverage was greatest, rather than after taking the reins.
In particular, he moved to secure the cooperation of the
hospital board by flatly stating his conditions for employment. He told the directors, for example, that
should they hire him, they could no longer interfere in
day-to-day management decisions. In his second and
third meetings with the board's search committee, Levy
laid out his timetable and intentions. He insisted that
the board decide on his appointment quickly so that he
could be on the job before the release of the Hunter report. He told the committee that he intended to push
for a smaller, more effective group of directors. Though

the conditions were somewhat unusual, the board was convinced that Levy had the experience to lead a successful turnaround, and they accepted his terms. Levy went to work on January 7, 2002.

The next task was to set the stage with the hospital staff. Levy was convinced that the employees, hungry for a turnaround, would do their best to cooperate with him if he could emulate and embody the core values of the hospital culture, rather than impose his personal values. He chose to act as the managerial equivalent of a good doctor—that is, as one who, in dealing with a very ill patient, delivers both the bad news and the chances of success honestly and imparts a realistic sense of hope, without sugar coating.

Like any leader facing a turnaround, Levy also knew he had to develop a bold message that provided compelling reasons to do things differently and then cast that message in capital letters to signal the arrival of a new order. To give his message teeth, he linked it to an implicit threat. Taking his cue from his private discussions with the state attorney general, whom he had persuaded to keep the hospital open for the time being, Levy chose to publicize the very real possibility the hospital would be sold. While he realized he risked frightening the staff and the patients with this bad news, he believed that a strong wake-up call was necessary to get employees to face up to the situation.

During his first morning on the job, Levy delivered an all-hands-on-deck e-mail to the staff. The memo contained four broad messages. It opened with the good news, pointing out that the organization had much to be proud of ("This is a wonderful institution, representing the very best in academic medicine: exemplary patient care, extraordinary research, and fine teaching"). Second, Levy noted that the threat of sale was real ("This is our last chance"). Third, he signaled the kinds of actions employees could expect him to take ("There will be a reduction in staff"). And finally, he described the open management style he would adopt. He would manage by walking around—lunching with staff in the cafeteria, having impromptu conversations in the hallways, talking with employees at every opportunity to discover their concerns. He would communicate directly with employees through e-mail rather than through intermediaries. He also noted that the Hunter report would be posted on the hospital intranet, where all employees would have the opportunity to review its recommendations and submit comments for the final turnaround plan. The direct, open tone of the e-mail memo signaled exactly how Levy's management style would differ from that of his predecessors.

In the afternoon, he disclosed BIDMC's situation in interviews with the *Boston Globe* and the *Boston Herald*, the city's two major newspapers. He told reporters the same thing he had told the hospital's employees: that, in the absence of a turnaround, the hospital would be sold to a for-profit chain and would therefore lose its status as a Harvard teaching hospital. Staving off a sale would require tough measures, including the laying off of anywhere from 500 to 700 employees. Levy insisted that there would be no nursing layoffs, in keeping with the hospital's core values of high-quality patient care. The newspaper reports, together with the memo circulated that morning, served to immediately reset employee expectations while dramatically increasing staff cooperation and willingness to accept whatever new initiatives might prove necessary to the hospital's survival.

Two days later, the critical Hunter report came out and was circulated via the hospital's intranet. Because the report had been produced by an objective third party, employees were open to its unvarnished, warts-and-all view of the hospital's current predicament. The facts were stark, and the staff could no longer claim ignorance. Levy received, and personally responded to, more than 300 e-mail suggestions for improvement in response to the report, many of which he later included in the turnaround plan.

Creating the Frame

Once the stage has been set for acceptance, effective leaders need to help employees interpret proposals for change. Complex plans can be interpreted in any number of ways; not all of them ensure acceptance and favorable outcomes. Skilled leaders therefore use "frames" to provide context and shape perspective for new proposals and plans. By framing the issues, leaders help people digest ideas in particular ways. A frame can take many forms: It can be a companywide presentation that prepares employees before an unexpected change, for example, or a radio interview that provides context following an unsettling layoff.

Levy used one particularly effective framing device to help employees interpret a preliminary draft of the turnaround plan. This device took the form of a detailed e-mail memo accompanying the dense, several-hundred-page plan. The memo explained, in considerable detail, the plan's purpose and expected impact.

The first section of the memo sought to mollify critics and reduce the fears of doctors and nurses. Its tone was positive and uplifting; it discussed BIDMC's mission, strategy, and uncompromising values, emphasizing the hospital's "warm, caring environment." This section of the letter also reaffirmed the importance of remaining an academic medical center, as well as reminding employees of their shared mission and ideals. The second part of the letter told employees what to expect, providing further details about the turnaround plan. It emphasized that tough measures and goals would be required but noted that the specific recommendations were based, for the most part, on the advice in the Hunter report, which employees had already reviewed. The message to employees was, "You've already seen and endorsed the Hunter report. There are no future surprises."

The third part of the letter anticipated and responded to prospective concerns; this had the effect of circumventing objections. This section explicitly diagnosed past plans and explained their deficiencies, which were largely due to their having been imposed top-down, with little employee ownership, buy-in, or discussion. Levy then offered a direct interpretation of what had gone wrong. Past plans, he said, had underestimated the size of the financial problem, set unrealistic expectations for new revenue growth, and failed to test implementation proposals. This section of the letter also drove home the need for change at a deeper, more visceral level than employees had experienced in the past. It emphasized that this plan was a far more collective effort than past proposals had been, because it incorporated many employee suggestions.

By framing the turnaround proposal this way, Levy accomplished two things. First, he was able to convince employees that the plan belonged to them. Second, the letter served as the basis for an ongoing communication platform. Levy reiterated its points at every opportunity—not only with employees but also in public meetings and in discussions with the press.

Managing the Mood

Turnarounds are depressing events, especially when they involve restructuring and downsizing. Relationships are disrupted, friends move on, and jobs disappear. In such settings, managing the mood of the organization becomes an essential leadership skill. Leaders must pay close attention to employees' emotions—the ebb and flow of their feelings and moods—and work hard to preserve a receptive climate for change. Often, this requires a delicate balancing act between presenting good and bad news in just the right proportion. Employees need to feel that their sacrifices have not been in vain and that their accomplishments have been recognized and rewarded. At the same time, they must be reminded that complacency is not an option. The communication challenge is daunting. One must strike the right notes of optimism and realism and carefully calibrate the timing, tone, and positioning of every message.

Paul Levy's challenge was threefold: to give remaining employees time to grieve and recover from layoffs and other difficult measures; to make them feel that he cared for and supported them; and to ensure that the turnaround plan proceeded apace. The process depended on mutual trust and employees' desire to succeed. "I had to calibrate the push and pull of congratulations and pressure, but I also depended on the staff's underlying value system and sense of mission," he said. "They were highly motivated, caring individuals who had stuck with the place through five years of hell. They wanted to do good."

The first step was to acknowledge employees' feelings of depression while helping them look to the future. Immediately after the first round of layoffs, people were feeling listless and dejected; Levy knew that releasing the final version of the turnaround plan too soon after the layoffs could be seen as cold. In an e-mail he sent to all employees a few days later, Levy explicitly empathized with employees' feelings ("This week is a sad one . . . it is hard for those of us remaining . . . offices are emptier than usual"). He then urged employees to look forward and concluded on a strongly optimistic note (". . . our target is not just survival: It is to thrive and set an example for what a unique academic medical center like ours means for this region"). His upbeat words were reinforced by a piece of good luck that weekend when the underdog New England Patriots won their first Super Bowl championship in dramatic fashion in the last 90 seconds of the game. When Levy returned to work the following Monday, employees were saying, "If the Patriots can do it, we can, too."

The next task was to keep employees focused on the continuing hard work ahead. On April 12, two months into the restructuring process, Levy sent out a "Frequently Asked Questions" e-mail giving a generally favorable view of progress to date. At the same time, he spoke plainly about the need to control costs and reminded employees that merit pay increases would remain on hold. This was hardly the rosy picture that most employees were hoping for, of course. But Levy believed sufficient time had passed that employees could accommodate a more realistic and tough tone on his part.

A month later, everything changed. Operational improvements that were put in place during the first phase of the turnaround had begun to take hold. Financial performance was well ahead of budget, with the best results since the merger. In another e-mail, Levy praised employees lavishly. He also convened a series of open question-and-answer forums, where employees heard more details about the hospital's tangible progress and received kudos for their accomplishments.

Reinforcing Good Habits

Without a doubt, the toughest challenge faced by leaders during a turnaround is to avoid backsliding into dysfunctional routines—habitual patterns of negative behavior by individuals and groups that are triggered automatically and unconsciously by familiar circumstances or stimuli. (For more on how such disruptive patterns work, see the exhibit "Dysfunctional Routines: Six Ways to Stop Change in Its Tracks.") Employees need help maintaining new behaviors, especially when their old ways of working are deeply ingrained and destructive. Effective change leaders provide opportunities for employees to practice desired behaviors repeatedly, while personally modeling new ways of working and providing coaching and support.

In our studies of successful turnarounds, we've found that effective leaders explicitly reinforce organizational values on a constant basis, using actions to back up their words. Their goal is to change behavior, not just ways of thinking. For example, a leader can talk about values such as openness, tolerance, civility, teamwork, delegation, and direct communication in meetings and e-mails. But the message takes hold only if he or she also signals a dislike of disruptive, divisive behaviors by pointedly—and, if necessary, publicly—criticizing them.

At Beth Israel Deaconess Medical Center, the chiefs of medicine, surgery, orthopedics, and other key functions presented Levy with special behavioral challenges, particularly because he was not a doctor. Each medical chief was in essence a "mini-dean," the head of a largely self-contained department with its own faculty, staff, and resources. As academic researchers, they were rewarded primarily for individual achievement. They had limited experience solving business or management problems.

In dealing with the chiefs, Levy chose an approach that blended with a strong dose of discipline with real-time, public reinforcement. He developed guidelines for behavior and insisted that everyone in the hospital measure up to them. In one of his earliest meetings with the chiefs, Levy presented a simple set of "meeting rules," including such chestnuts as "state your objections" and "disagree without being disagreeable," and led a discussion about them, demonstrating the desired behaviors through his own leadership of the meeting. The purpose of these rules was to introduce new standards of inter-personal behavior and, in the process, to combat several dysfunctional routines.

One serious test of Levy's ability to reinforce these norms came a month and a half after he was named CEO. After a staff meeting at which all the department chairs were present, one chief—who had remained silent—sent an e-mail to Levy complaining about a decision made during the meeting. The e-mail copied the other chiefs as well as the chairman of the board. Many CEOs would choose to criticize such behavior privately. But Levy responded in an e-mail to the same audience, publicly denouncing the chief for his tone, his lack of

Dysfunctional Routines

Six Ways to Stop Change in Its Tracks

Just as people are creatures of habit, organizations thrive on routines. Management teams, for example, routinely cut budgets after performance deviates from plan. Routines—predictable, virtually automatic behaviors—are unstated, self-reinforcing, and remarkably resilient. Because they lead to more efficient cognitive processing, they are, for the most part, functional and highly desirable.

Dysfunctional routines, by contrast, are barriers to action and change. Some are outdated behaviors that were appropriate once but are now unhelpful. Others manifest themselves in knee-jerk reactions, passivity, unproductive foot-dragging, and, sometimes, active resistance.

Dysfunctional routines are persistent, but they are not unchangeable. Novelty—the perception that current circumstances are truly different from those that previously prevailed—is one of the most potent forces for dislodging routines. To overcome them, leaders must clearly signal that the context has changed. They must work directly with employees to recognize and publicly examine dysfunctional routines and substitute desired behaviors.

A culture of "no."

In organizations dominated by cynics and critics, there is always a good reason not to do something. Piling on criticism is an easy way to avoid taking risks and claim false superiority. Lou Gerstner gets credit for naming this routine, which he found on his arrival at IBM, but it is common in many organizations. Another CEO described her team's response to new initiatives by likening it to a skeet shoot. "Someone would yell, 'Pull!', there would be a deafening blast, and the idea would be in pieces on the ground." This routine has two sources: a culture that overvalues criticism and analysis, and complex decision-making processes requiring multiple approvals, in which anybody can say "no" but nobody can say "yes." It is especially likely in organizations that are divided into large subunits or segments, led by local

---

civility, and his failure to speak up earlier in the process, as required by the new meeting rules. It was as close to a public hanging as anyone could get. Several of the chiefs privately expressed their support to Levy; they too had been offended by their peer's presumptuousness. More

leaders with great power who are often unwilling to comply with directives from above.

The dog and pony show must go on.
Some organizations put so much weight on process that they confuse ends and means, form and content. How you present a proposal becomes more important than what you propose. Managers construct presentations carefully and devote large amounts of time to obtaining sign-offs. The result is death by PowerPoint. Despite the appearance of progress, there's little real headway.

The grass is always greener.
To avoid facing challenges in their core business, some managers look to new products, new services, and new lines of business. At times, such diversification is healthy. But all too often these efforts are merely an avoidance tactic that keeps tough problems at arm's length.

After the meeting ends, debate begins.
This routine is often hard to spot because so much of it takes place under cover. Cordial, apparently cooperative meetings are followed by resistance. Sometimes, resisters are covert; often, they end-run established forums entirely and take their concerns directly to the top. The result? Politics triumphs over substance, staff meetings become empty rituals, and meddling becomes the norm.

Ready, aim, aim . . .
Here, the problem is the organization's inability to settle on a definitive course of action. Staff members generate a continual stream of proposals and reports; managers repeatedly tinker with each one, fine-tuning their choices without ever making a final decision. Often called "analysis paralysis," this pattern is common in perfectionist cultures where mistakes are career threatening and people who rock the boat drown.

This too shall pass.
In organizations where prior leaders repeatedly proclaimed a state of crisis but then made few substantive changes, employees tend to be jaded. In such situations, they develop a heads-down, bunker mentality and a reluctance to respond to management directives. Most believe that the wisest course of action is to ignore new initiatives, work around them, or wait things out.

---

broadly, the open criticism served to powerfully reinforce new norms while curbing disruptive behavior.

Even as they must set expectations and reinforce behaviors, effective change leaders also recognize that many employees simply do not know how to make decisions as

a group or work cooperatively. By delegating critical decisions and responsibilities, a leader can provide employees
with ample opportunities to practice new ways of working; in such cases, employees' performance should be
evaluated as much on their adherence to the new standards and processes as on their substantive choices. In
this spirit, Levy chose to think of himself primarily as a
kind of appeals court judge. When employees came to
him seeking his intervention on an issue or situation, he
explained, he would "review the process used by the
'lower court' to determine if it followed the rules. If so, the
decision stands." He did not review cases de novo and
substitute his judgment for that of the individual department or unit. He insisted that employees work through
difficult issues themselves, even when they were not so in-
clined, rather than rely on him to tell them what to do. At
other times, he intervened personally and coached employees when they lacked basic skills. When two members
of his staff disagreed on a proposed course of action, Levy
triggered an open, emotional debate, then worked with
the participants and their bosses behind the scenes to resolve the differences. At the next staff meeting, he praised
the participants' willingness to disagree publicly, reem-
phasizing that vigorous debate was healthy and desirable
and that confrontation was not to be avoided. In this way,
employees gained experience in working through their
problems on their own.

Performance, of course, is the ultimate measure of a
successful turnaround. On that score, BIDMC has done
exceedingly well since Levy took the helm. The original
restructuring plan called for a three-year improvement
process, moving from a $58 million loss in 2001 to
breakeven in 2004. At the end of the 2004 fiscal year, performance was far ahead of plan, with the hospital report-

ing a $37.4 million net gain from operations. Revenues were up, while costs were sharply reduced. Decision making was now crisper and more responsive, even though there was little change in the hospital's senior staff or medical leadership. Morale, not surprisingly, was up as well. To take just one indicator, annual nursing turnover, which was 15% to 16% when Levy became CEO, had dropped to 3% by mid-2004. Pleased with the hospital's performance, the board signed Levy to a new three-year contract.

Heads, Hearts, and Hands

It's clear that the key to Paul Levy's success at Beth Israel Deaconess Medical Center is that he understood the importance of making sure the cultural soil had been made ready before planting the seeds of change. In a receptive environment, employees not only understand why change is necessary; they're also emotionally committed to making it happen, and they faithfully execute the required steps.

On a cognitive level, employees in receptive environments are better able to let go of competing, unsubstantiated views of the nature and extent of the problems facing their organizations. They hold the same, objective views of the causes of poor performance. They acknowledge the seriousness of current financial, operational, and marketplace difficulties. And they take responsibility for their own contributions to those problems. Such a shared, fact-based diagnosis is crucial for moving forward.

On an emotional level, employees in receptive environments identify with the organization and its values and are committed to its continued existence. They believe that the organization stands for something more than profitability, market share, or stock performance and is therefore worth saving. Equally important, they trust the leader, believing that he or she shares their values and will fight to preserve them. Leaders earn considerable latitude from employees—and their proposals usually get the benefit of the doubt—when their hearts are thought to be in the right place.

Workers in such environments also have physical, hands-on experience with the new behaviors expected of them. They have seen the coming changes up close and understand what they are getting into. In such an atmosphere where it's acceptable for employees to wrestle with decisions on their own and practice unfamiliar ways of working, a leader can successfully allay irrational fears and undercut the myths that so often accompany major change efforts.

There is a powerful lesson in all this for leaders. To create a receptive environment, persuasion is the ultimate tool. Persuasion promotes understanding; understanding breeds acceptance; acceptance leads to action. Without persuasion, even the best of turnaround plans will fail to take root.

Originally published in February 2005
Reprint R0502F

Moments of Greatness

Entering the Fundamental State of Leadership

ROBERT E. QUINN

Executive Summary

WHEN WE DO OUR BEST WORK AS LEADERS, we don't imitate others. Rather, we draw on our own values and capabilities. We enter what author Robert Quinn calls the *fundamental state of leadership*. This is a frame of mind we tend to adopt when facing a significant challenge: a promotion opportunity, the risk of professional failure, a serious illness, a divorce, the death of a loved one, or any other major life jolt. Crisis calls, and we rise to the occasion.

But we don't need to spend time in the dark night of the soul to reach this fundamental state. We can make the shift at any time by asking ourselves—and honestly answering—four transformative questions:

Am I results centered? (Am I willing to leave my comfort zone to make things happen?)

Am I internally directed? (Am I behaving according to my values rather than bending to social or political pressures?)

Am I other focused? (Am I putting the collective good above my own needs?)

Am I externally open? (Am I receptive to outside stimuli that may signal the need for change?)

When we can answer these questions in the affirmative, we're prepared to lead in the truest sense.

Of course, we can't sustain the fundamental state of leadership indefinitely. Fatigue and external resistance pull us out of it. But each time we reach it, we then return to our everyday selves a bit more capable, and we usually boost the performance of the people around us. Over time, we create a high-performance culture—and that *can* be sustained.

As leaders, sometimes we're truly "on," and sometimes we're not. Why is that? What separates the episodes of excellence from those of mere competence? In striving to tip the balance toward excellence, we try to identify great leaders' qualities and behaviors so we can develop them ourselves. Nearly all corporate training programs and books on leadership are grounded in the assumption that we should study the behaviors of those who have been successful and teach people to emulate them.

But my colleagues and I have found that when leaders do their best work, they don't copy anyone. Instead, they draw on their own fundamental values and capabilities—operating in a frame of mind that is true to them yet, paradoxically, not their normal state of being. I call it the *fundamental state of leadership*. It's the way we lead when we encounter a crisis and finally choose to move forward. Think back to a time when you faced a significant life challenge: a promotion opportunity, the risk of professional failure, a serious illness, a divorce, the death of a loved one, or any other major jolt. Most likely, if you made decisions not to meet others' expectations but to suit what you instinctively understood to be right—in other words, if you were at your very best—you rose to the task because you were being tested.

Is it possible to enter the fundamental state of leadership without crisis? In my work coaching business executives, I've found that if we ask ourselves—and honestly answer—just four questions, we can make the shift at any time. It's a temporary state. Fatigue and external resistance pull us out of it. But each time we reach it, we return to our everyday selves a bit more capable, and we usually elevate the performance of the people around us as well. Over time, we all can become more effective leaders by deliberately choosing to enter the fundamental state of leadership rather than waiting for crisis to force us there.

Defining the Fundamental State

Even those who are widely admired for their seemingly easy and natural leadership skills—presidents, prime ministers, CEOs—do not usually function in the fundamental state of leadership. Most of the time, they are in their normal state—a healthy and even necessary condition under many circumstances, but not one that's conducive to coping with crisis. In the normal state, people tend to stay within their comfort zones and allow external forces to direct their behaviors and decisions. They lose moral influence and often rely on rational argument and the exercise of authority to bring about change. Others comply with what these leaders ask, out of fear, but the result is usually unimaginative and incremental—and largely reproduces what already exists.

To elevate the performance of others, we must elevate ourselves into the fundamental state of leadership. Getting there requires a shift along four dimensions. (See the exhibit "There's Normal, and There's Fundamental.")

First, we move from being comfort centered to being results centered. The former feels safe but eventually leads to a sense of languishing and meaninglessness. In

---

There's Normal, and There's Fundamental

Under everyday circumstances, leaders can remain in their normal state of being and do what they need to do. But some challenges require a heightened perspective—what can be called the fundamental state of leadership. Here's how the two states differ.

In the normal state, I am . . .	**In the fundamental state, I am . . .**
Comfort centered	**Results centered**
I stick with what I know.	I venture beyond familiar territory to pursue ambitious new outcomes.
Externally directed	**Internally directed**
I comply with others' wishes in an effort to keep the peace.	I behave according to my values.
Self-focused	**Other focused**
I place my interests above those of the group.	I put the collective good first.
Internally closed	**Externally open**
I block out external stimuli in order to stay on task and avoid risk.	I learn from my environment and recognize when there's a need for change.

his book *The Path of Least Resistance*, Robert Fritz carefully explains how asking a single question can move us from the normal, reactive state to a much more generative condition. That question is this: What result do I want to create? Giving an honest answer pushes us off nature's path of least resistance. It leads us from problem solving to purpose finding.

Second, we move from being externally directed to being more internally directed. That means that we stop merely complying with others' expectations and conforming to the current culture. To become more internally directed is to clarify our core values and increase our integrity, confidence, and authenticity. As we become more confident and more authentic, we behave differently. Others must make sense of our new behavior. Some will be attracted to it, and some will be offended by it. That's not prohibitive, though: When we are true to our values, we are willing to initiate such conflict.

Third, we become less self-focused and more focused on others. We put the needs of the organization as a whole above our own. Few among us would admit that personal needs trump the collective good, but the impulse to control relationships in a way that feeds our own interests is natural and normal. That said, self-focus over time leads to feelings of isolation. When we put the collective good first, others reward us with their trust and respect. We form tighter, more sensitive bonds. Empathy increases, and cohesion follows. We create an enriched sense of community, and that helps us transcend the conflicts that are a necessary element in high-performing organizations.

Fourth, we become more open to outside signals or stimuli, including those that require us to do things we are not comfortable doing. In the normal state, we pay attention to signals that we know to be relevant. If they suggest incremental adjustments, we respond. If, however, they call for more dramatic changes, we may adopt a posture of defensiveness and denial; this mode of self-protection and self-deception separates us from the ever-changing external world. We live according to an outdated, less valid, image of what is real. But in the fundamental state of leadership, we are more aware of what is unfolding, and we generate new images all the time. We are adaptive, credible, and unique. In this externally open state, no two people are alike.

These four qualities—being results centered, internally directed, other focused, and externally open—are at the heart of positive human influence, which is generative and attractive. A person without these four characteristics can also be highly influential, but his or her influence tends to be predicated on some form of control or force, which does not usually give rise to committed followers. By entering the fundamental state of leadership, we increase the likelihood of attracting others to an elevated level of community, a high-performance state that may continue even when we are not present.

Preparing for the Fundamental State

Because people usually do not leave their comfort zones unless forced, many find it helpful to follow a process when they choose to enter the fundamental state of leadership. I teach a technique to executives and use it in my own work. It simply involves asking four awareness-raising questions designed to help us transcend our natural denial mechanisms. When people become aware of their hypocrisies, they are more likely to change. Those who are new to the "fundamental state" concept, however, need to take two preliminary steps before they can understand and employ it.

Step 1: Recognize that you have previously entered the fundamental state of leadership. Every reader of this publication has reached, at one time or another, the fundamental state of leadership. We've all faced a great personal or professional challenge and spent time in the dark night of the soul. In successfully working through such episodes, we inevitably enter the fundamental state of leadership.

When I introduce people to this concept, I ask them to identify two demanding experiences from their past and ponder what happened in terms of intention, integrity, trust, and adaptability. At first, they resist the exercise because I am asking them to revisit times of great personal pain. But as they recount their experiences, they begin to see that they are also returning to moments of greatness. Our painful experiences often bring out our best selves. Recalling the lessons of such moments releases positive emotions and makes it easier to see what's possible in the present. In this exercise, I ask people to consider their behavior during these episodes in relation to the characteristics of the fundamental state of leadership. (See the exhibit "You've Already Been There" for analyses of two actual episodes.)

Sometimes I also ask workshop participants to share their stories with one another. Naturally, they are reluctant to talk about such dark moments. To help people open up, I share my own moments of great challenge, the ones I would normally keep to myself. By exhibiting vulnerability, I'm able to win the group's trust and embolden other people to exercise the same courage. I recently ran a workshop with a cynical group of

You've Already Been There

Two participants in a leadership workshop at the University of Michigan's Ross School of Business used this self-assessment tool to figure out how they've transcended their greatest life challenges by entering the fundamental state of leadership. You can use the same approach in analyzing how you've conquered your most significant challenges.

	Participant A	Participant B
The pivotal crisis:	I was thrust into a job that was crucial to the organization but greatly exceeded my capabilities. I had to get people to do things they did not want to do.	I was driving myself hard at work, and things kept getting worse at home. Finally my wife told me she wanted a divorce.
How did you become more results centered?	I kept trying to escape doing what was required, but I could not stand the guilt. I finally decided I had to change. I envisioned what success might look like, and I committed to making whatever changes were necessary.	I felt I'd lost everything: family, wealth, and stature. I withdrew from relationships. I started drinking heavily. I finally sought professional help for my sorrow and, with guidance, clarified my values and made choices about my future.

How did you become more internally directed?	I stopped worrying so much about how other people would evaluate and judge me. I was starting to operate from my own values. I felt more self-empowered than ever and realized how fear driven I had been.	I engaged in a lot of self-reflection and journal writing. It became clear that I was not defined by marriage, wealth, or stature. I was more than that. I began to focus on how I could make a difference for other people. I got more involved in my community.
How did you become more focused on others?	I realized how much I needed people, and I became more concerned about them. I was better able to hear what they were saying. I talked not just from my head but also from my heart. My colleagues responded. Today, I am still close to those people.	As I started to grow and feel more self-confident, I became better at relating. At work, I now ask more of people than I ever did before, but I also give them far more support. I care about them, and they can tell.
How did you become more externally open?	I experimented with new approaches. They often did not work, but they kept the brainstorming in motion. I paid attention to every kind of feedback. I was hungry to get it right. There was a lot of discovery. Each step forward was exhilarating.	I began to feel stronger. I was less intimidated when people gave me negative feedback. I think it was because I was less afraid of changing and growing.

executives. After I broke the testimonial ice, one of the participants told us of a time when he had accepted a new job that required him to relocate his family. Just before he was to start, his new boss called in a panic, asking him to cut his vacation short and begin work immediately. The entire New England engineering team had quit; clients in the region had no support whatsoever. The executive started his job early, and his family had to navigate the move without his help. He described the next few months as "the worst and best experience" of his life.

Another executive shared that he'd found out he had cancer the same week he was promoted and relocated to Paris, not knowing how to speak French. His voice cracked as he recalled these stressful events. But then he told us about the good that came out of them—how he conquered both the disease and the job while also becoming a more authentic and influential leader.

Others came forward with their own stories, and I saw a great change in the group. The initial resistance and cynicism began to disappear, and participants started exploring the fundamental state of leadership in a serious way. They saw the power in the concept and recognized that hiding behind their pride or reputation would only get in the way of future progress. In recounting their experiences, they came to realize that they had become more purposive, authentic, compassionate, and responsive.

Step 2: Analyze your current state. When we're in the fundamental state, we take on various positive characteristics, such as clarity of vision, self-empowerment, empathy, and creative thinking. (See the exhibit "Are You in the Fundamental State of Leadership?" for a

Are You in the Fundamental State of Leadership?

Think of a time when you reached the fundamental state of leadership—that is, when you were at your best as a leader—and use this checklist to identify the qualities you displayed. Then check off the items that describe your behavior today. Compare the past and present. If there's a significant difference, what changes do you need to make to get back to the fundamental state?

At my best I was . . .	Today I am . . .	
		Results centered
_____	_____	Knowing what result I'd like to create
_____	_____	Holding high standards
_____	_____	Initiating actions
_____	_____	Challenging people
_____	_____	Disrupting the status quo
_____	_____	Capturing people's attention
_____	_____	Feeling a sense of shared purpose
_____	_____	Engaging in urgent conversations
		Internally directed
_____	_____	Operating from my core values
_____	_____	Finding motivation from within
_____	_____	Feeling self-empowered
_____	_____	Leading courageously
_____	_____	Bringing hidden conflicts to the surface
_____	_____	Expressing what I really believe
_____	_____	Feeling a sense of shared reality
_____	_____	Engaging in authentic conversations
		Other focused
_____	_____	Sacrificing personal interests for the common good
_____	_____	Seeing the potential in everyone
_____	_____	Trusting others and fostering interdependence
_____	_____	Empathizing with people's needs
_____	_____	Expressing concern
_____	_____	Supporting people
_____	_____	Feeling a sense of shared identity
_____	_____	Engaging in participative conversations
		Externally open
_____	_____	Moving forward into uncertainty
_____	_____	Inviting feedback
_____	_____	Paying deep attention to what's unfolding
_____	_____	Learning exponentially
_____	_____	Watching for new opportunities
_____	_____	Growing continually
_____	_____	Feeling a sense of shared contribution
_____	_____	Engaging in creative conversations

checklist organized along the four dimensions.) Most of us would like to say we display these characteristics at all times, but we really do so only sporadically.

Comparing our normal performance with what we have done at our very best often creates a desire to elevate what we are doing now. Knowing we've operated at a higher level in the past instills confidence that we can do so again; it quells our fear of stepping into unknown and risky territory.

Asking Four Transformative Questions

Of course, understanding the fundamental state of leadership and recognizing its power are not the same as being there. Entering that state is where the real work comes in. To get started, we can ask ourselves four questions that correspond with the four qualities of the fundamental state.

To show how each of these qualities affects our behavior while we're in the fundamental state of leadership, I'll draw on stories from two executives. One is a company president; we'll call him John Jones. The other, Robert Yamamoto, is the executive director of the Los Angeles Junior Chamber of Commerce. Both once struggled with major challenges that changed the way they thought about their jobs and their lives.

I met John in an executive course I was teaching. He was a successful change leader who had turned around two companies in his corporation. Yet he was frustrated. He had been promised he'd become president of the largest company in the corporation as soon as the current president retired, which would happen in the near future. In the meantime, he had been told to bide his time with a company that everyone considered dead. His assignment was simply to oversee the funeral, yet he took it as a personal challenge to turn the company around. After he had been there nine months, however, there was little improvement, and the people were still not very engaged.

As for Robert, he had been getting what he considered to be acceptable (if not exceptional) results in his company. So when the new board president asked him to prepare a letter of resignation, Robert was stunned. He underwent a period of anguished introspection, during which he began to distrust others and question his own management skills and leadership ability. Concerned for his family and his future, he started to seek another job and wrote the requested letter.

As you will see, however, even though things looked grim for both Robert and John, they were on the threshold of positive change.

AM I RESULTS CENTERED?

Most of the time, we are comfort centered. We try to continue doing what we know how to do. We may think we are pursuing new outcomes, but if achieving them means leaving our comfort zones, we subtly—even unconsciously—find ways to avoid doing so. We typically advocate ambitious outcomes while designing our work for maximum administrative convenience, which allows us to avoid conflict but frequently ends up reproducing what already exists. Often, others collude with us to act out this deception. Being comfort centered is hypocritical, self-deceptive, and normal.

Clarifying the result we want to create requires us to reorganize our lives. Instead of moving away from a problem, we move toward a possibility that does not yet exist. We become more proactive, intentional, optimistic, invested, and persistent. We also tend to become more energized, and our impact on others becomes energizing.

Consider what happened with John. When I first spoke with him, he sketched out his strategy with little enthusiasm. Sensing that lack of passion, I asked him a question designed to test his commitment to the end he claimed he wanted to obtain:

> *What if you told your people the truth? Suppose you told them that nobody really expects you to succeed, that you were assigned to be a caretaker for 18 months, and that you have been promised a plum job once your assignment is through. And then you tell them that you have chosen instead to give up that plum job and bet your career on the people present. Then, from your newly acquired stance of optimism for the company's prospects, you issue some challenges beyond your employees' normal capacity.*

To my surprise, John responded that he was beginning to think along similar lines. He grabbed a napkin and rapidly sketched out a new strategy along with a plan for carrying it out, including reassignments for his staff. It was clear and compelling, and he was suddenly full of energy.

What happened here? John was the president of his company and therefore had authority. And he'd turned around two other companies—evidence that he had the knowledge and competencies of a change leader. Yet he was failing as a change leader. That's because he had slipped into his comfort zone. He was going through the motions, doing what had worked elsewhere. He was imitating a great leader—in this case, John himself. But imitation is not the way to enter the fundamental state of leadership. If I had accused John of not being committed to a real vision, he would have been incensed. He would have argued heatedly in denial of the truth. All I had to do, though, was nudge him in the right direction. As soon as he envisioned the result he wanted to create and committed himself to it, a new strategy emerged and he was reenergized.

Then there was Robert, who went to what he assumed would be his last board meeting and found that he had more support than he'd been led to believe. Shockingly, at the end of the meeting, he still had his job. Even so, this fortuitous turn brought on further soul-searching. Robert started to pay more attention to what he was doing; he began to see his tendency to be tactical and to gravitate toward routine tasks. He concluded that he was managing, not leading. He was playing a role and abdicating leadership to the board president—not because that person had the knowledge and vision to lead but because the position came with the statutory right to lead. "I suddenly decided to really lead my organization," Robert said. "It was as if a new person emerged. The decision was not about me. I needed to do it for the good of the organization."

In deciding to "really lead," Robert started identifying the strategic outcomes he wanted to create. As he did this, he found himself leaving his zone of comfort— behaving in new ways and generating new outcomes.

AM I INTERNALLY DIRECTED?

In the normal state, we comply with social pressures in order to avoid conflict and remain connected with our coworkers. However, we end up feeling *less* connected because conflict avoidance results in political compromise.

We begin to lose our uniqueness and our sense of integrity. The agenda gradually shifts from creating an external result to preserving political peace. As this problem intensifies, we begin to lose hope and energy.

This loss was readily apparent in the case of John. He was his corporation's shining star. But since he was at least partially focused on the future reward—the plum job—he was not fully focused on doing the hard work he needed to do at the moment. So he didn't ask enough of the people he was leading. To get more from them, John needed to be more internally directed.

AM I OTHER FOCUSED?

It's hard to admit, but most of us, most of the time, put our own needs above those of the whole. Indeed, it is healthy to do so; it's a survival mechanism. But when the pursuit of our own interests controls our relationships, we erode others' trust in us. Although people may comply with our wishes, they no longer derive energy from their relationships with us. Over time we drive away the very social support we seek.

To become more focused on others is to commit to the collective good in relationships, groups, or organizations, even if it means incurring personal costs. When John made the shift into the fundamental state of leadership, he committed to an uncertain future for himself. He had been promised a coveted job. All he had to do was wait a few months. Still, he was unhappy, so he chose to turn down the opportunity in favor of a course that was truer to his leadership values. When he shifted gears, he sacrificed his personal security in favor of a greater good.

Remember Robert's words: "The decision was not about me. I needed to do it for the good of the organization." After entering the fundamental state of leadership, he proposed a new strategic direction to the board's president and said that if the board didn't like it, he would walk away with no regrets. He knew that the strategy would benefit the organization, regardless of how it would affect him personally. Robert put the good of the organization first. When a leader does this, people notice, and the leader gains respect and trust. Group members, in turn, become more likely to put the collective good first. When they do, tasks that previously seemed impossible become doable.

AM I EXTERNALLY OPEN?

Being closed to external stimuli has the benefit of keeping us on task, but it also allows us to ignore signals that suggest a need for change. Such signals would force us to cede control and face risk, so denying them is self-protective, but it is also self-deceptive. John convinced himself he'd done all he could for his failing company when, deep down, he knew that he had the capacity to improve things. Robert was self-deceptive, too, until crisis and renewed opportunity caused him to open up and explore the fact that he was playing a role accorded him but not using his knowledge and emotional capacity to transcend that role and truly lead his people.

Asking ourselves whether we're externally open shifts our focus from controlling our environment to learning from it and helps us recognize the need for change. Two things happen as a result. First, we are forced to improvise in response to previously unrecognized cues—that is, to depart from established routines. And second, because trial-and-error survival requires an accurate picture of the results we're creating, we actively and genuinely seek honest feedback. Since people trust us more when we're in this state, they tend to offer more accurate feedback, understanding that we are likely to learn from the message rather than kill the messenger. A cycle of learning and empowerment is created, allowing us to see things that people normally cannot see and to formulate transformational strategies.

Applying the Fundamental Principles

Just as I teach others about the fundamental state of leadership, I also try to apply the concept in my own life. I was a team leader on a project for the University of Michigan's Executive Education Center. Usually, the center runs weeklong courses that bring in 30 to 40 executives. It was proposed that we develop a new product, an integrated week of perspectives on leadership. C.K. Prahalad would begin with a strategic perspective, then Noel Tichy, Dave Ulrich, Karl Weick, and I would follow with our own presentations. The objective was to fill a 400-seat auditorium. Since each presenter had a reasonably large following in some domain of the executive world, we were confident we could fill the seats, so we scheduled the program for the month of July, when our facilities were typically underutilized.

In the early months of planning and organizing, everything went perfectly. A marketing consultant had said we could expect to secure half our enrollment three weeks prior to the event. When that time rolled around, slightly less than half of the target audience had signed up, so we thought all was well. But then a different consultant indicated that for our kind of event we would get few additional enrollments during the last three weeks. This stunning prediction meant that attendance would be half of what we expected and we would be lucky to break even.

As the team leader, I could envision the fallout. Our faculty members, accustomed to drawing a full house, would be offended by a half-empty room; the dean would want to know what went wrong; and the center's staff would probably point to the team leader as the problem. That night I spent several hours pacing the floor. I was filled with dread and shame. Finally I told myself that this kind of behavior was useless. I went to my desk and wrote down the four questions. As I considered them, I concluded that I was comfort centered, externally directed, self-focused, and internally closed.

So I asked myself, "What result do I want to create?" I wrote that I wanted the center to learn how to offer a new, world-class product that would be in demand over time. With that clarification came a freeing insight: Because this was our first offering of the product, turning a large profit was not essential. That would be nice, of course, but we'd be happy to learn how to do such an event properly, break even, and lay the groundwork for making a profit in the future.

I then asked myself, "How can I become other focused?" At that moment, I was totally self-focused—I was worried about my reputation—and my first inclination was to be angry with the staff. But in shifting my focus to what they might be thinking that night, I realized they were most likely worried that I'd come to work in the morning ready to assign blame. Suddenly, I saw a need to both challenge and support them.

Finally, I thought about how I could become externally open. It would mean moving forward and learning something new, even if that made me uncomfortable. I needed to engage in an exploratory dialogue rather than preside as the expert in charge.

I immediately began making a list of marketing strategies, though I expected many of them would prove foolish since I knew nothing about marketing. The next day, I brought the staff together—and they, naturally, were guarded. I asked them what result we wanted to create. What happened next is a good example of how contagious the fundamental state of leadership can be.

We talked about strategies for increasing attendance, and after a while, I told the staff that I had some silly marketing ideas and was embarrassed to share them but was willing to do anything to help. They laughed at many of my naive thoughts about how to increase publicity and create pricing incentives. Yet my proposals also sparked serious discussion, and the group began to brainstorm its way into a collective strategy. Because I was externally open, there was space and time for everyone to lead. People came up with better ways of approaching media outlets and creating incentives. In that meeting, the group developed a shared sense of purpose, reality, identity, and contribution. They left feeling reasonable optimism and went forward as a committed team.

In the end, we did not get 400 participants, but we filled more than enough seats to have a successful event. We more than broke even, and we developed the skills we needed to run such an event better in the future. The program was a success because something transformational occurred among the staff. Yet the transformation did not originate in the meeting. It began the night before, when I asked myself the four questions and moved from the normal, reactive state to the fundamental state of leadership. And my entry into the fundamental state encouraged the staff to enter as well.

While the fundamental state proves useful in times of crisis, it can also help us cope with more mundane challenges. If I am going to have an important conversation, attend a key meeting, participate in a significant event, or teach a class, part of my preparation is to try to reach the fundamental state of leadership. Whether I am working with an individual, a group, or an organization, I ask the same four questions. They often lead to high-performance outcomes, and the repetition of high-performance outcomes can eventually create a high-performance culture.

Inspiring Others to High Performance

When we enter the fundamental state of leadership, we immediately have new thoughts and engage in new behaviors. We can't remain in this state forever. It can last for hours, days, or sometimes months, but eventually we come back to our normal frame of mind. While the fundamental state is temporary, each time we are in it we learn more about people and our environment and increase the probability that we will be able to return to it. Moreover, we inspire those around us to higher levels of performance.

To this day, Robert marvels at the contrast between his organization's past and present. His transformation into a leader with positive energy and a willingness and ability to tackle challenges in new ways helped shape the L.A. Junior Chamber of Commerce into a high-functioning and creative enterprise. When I last spoke to Robert, here's what he had to say:

> *I have a critical mass of individuals on both the staff and the board who are willing to look at our challenges in a new way and work on solutions together. At our meetings, new energy is present. What previously seemed unimaginable now seems to happen with ease.*

Any CEO would be delighted to be able to say these things. But the truth is, it's not a typical situation. When Robert shifted into the fundamental state of leadership, his group (which started off in a normal state) came to life, infused with his renewed energy and vision. Even after he'd left the fundamental state, the group sustained a higher level of performance. It continues to flourish, without significant staff changes or restructuring.

All this didn't happen because Robert read a book or an article about the best practices of some great leader. It did not happen because he was imitating someone else. It happened because he was jolted out of his comfort zone and was forced to enter the fundamental state of leadership. He was driven to clarify the result he wanted to create, to act courageously from his core values, to surrender his self-interest to the collective good, and to open himself up to learning in real time. From Robert, and others like him, we can learn the value of challenging ourselves in this way—a painful process but one with great potential to make a positive impact on our own lives and on the people around us.

Originally published in July–August 2005
Reprint R0507F

Change Without Pain

ERIC ABRAHAMSON

Executive Summary

CHANGE OR PERISH IS A CORPORATE TRUISM, but so is its unhappy corollary: many companies change *and* perish. The process of change can tear an organization apart. Drawing on his research over ten years, the author suggests that companies alternate major change initiatives with carefully paced periods of smaller, organic change using processes he calls *tinkering* and *kludging* (kludging is tinkering on large scale). The result is *dynamic stability,* which allows change without fatal pain.

Citing examples from General Electric to Barnesandnoble.com, the author describes dynamic stability as a process of continual but relatively small reconfigurations of existing practices and business models rather than the creation of new ones.

As they tinker and kludge, successful companies would be wise to follow these four guidelines: reward

shameless borrowing; appoint a chief memory officer
who can help the company avoid making the same old
mistakes; tinker and kludge internally before searching for
solutions externally; and hire generalists, because generalists tend to be more adept at tinkering and kludging.

As a paradigm of successful pacing, the author cites
the efforts of Lou Gerstner at IBM, American Express
Travel Related Services, and RJR Nabisco. Initially,
Gerstner engineered rapid, disruptive change at each
company, but he had a genius for knowing when it was
time to rest. He was alert to signs of cynicism and burnout.
Oscillation between big changes and small changes
helps ensure dynamic stability in organizations. More important, it paves the way for change that succeeds.

W<small>HO HASN'T HEARD THE MANTRA:</small> change or perish? It's a corporate cliché by now. And like many clichés,
it happens to be true. But so, too, is its unhappy corollary: many companies change and perish. Change is so
disruptive it can tear organizations apart.

Over the past ten years, I have been studying how
companies change, and my research suggests a counter-
intuitive imperative. To change successfully, companies
should stop changing all the time. Instead, they should
intersperse major change initiatives among carefully
paced periods of smaller, organic change, using processes I call *tinkering* and *kludging*. By doing so, companies can manage overall change with an approach called
dynamic stability. To be sure, achieving dynamic stability
is more difficult than ramming big, hairy, audacious
changes through an organization, in much the same way
that it is more difficult to end a war with negotiations
than with an atomic bomb. But dynamic stability has the

great advantage of leaving survivors. It allows change without fatal pain.

The Problem with Change

Change, as it is usually orchestrated, creates initiative overload and organizational chaos, both of which provoke strong resistance from the people most affected. Traveling from company to company in my research, I repeatedly encountered more and more "permafrost" organizations, where change-fatigued middle managers froze out initiatives introduced by the 20-somethings below them and the senior managers above them who were hot for change.

Their resistance found its voice in an aggressive cynicism. People spoke about change programs in angry, often offensive language, and *Dilbert* cartoons festooned almost every office door. As one middle manager put it, his company's change initiatives proved the first law of corporate physics: when the pendulum swings, don't stick your neck out. Employees greeted each new change program with a companywide "BOHICA" alert—bend over, here it comes again.

The change programs in question here—programs that have been all the rage since the 1970s—typically involve drastic measures as CEOs seek to maximize growth or economic value as quickly as possible. In dynamic stability, by contrast, the goal is change that can be sustained over both the short and long term. Let's consider two cases. The first involves Finley, Kumble, Wagner, Heine, Underberg, Manley, Myerson & Casey, a New York City-based law firm that tried to globalize at breakneck speed. The second is the story of General Electric, a company well known for its successful transformation, which owes much—in my analysis—to dynamic stability.

In its drive to become a global competitor, Finley Kumble speedily added partners and associates throughout the 1980s. Its commitment to rapid growth was epitomized by the words of Stephen Kumble, one of the lead partners: "I can take about five minutes of my wife. I can stand to read only one chapter of a book. I can't get through the first act of a play. All I think about is getting business." These words echo the 24/7 rhetoric of the e-commerce world. But the firm's pace wasn't sustainable. Finley Kumble collapsed in 1988 amid huge debts, vicious internecine conflict, and numerous legal improprieties. As Shakespeare said, "They stumble that run fast."

General Electric, by contrast, wanted rapid change, but it also knew when to slow down. Throughout the 1980s, GE engaged in creative—most people would say brutal—destruction involving massive layoffs, restructuring, and divestitures. But GE's changes in the 1990s—boundarylessness, six sigma quality, service additions to products—have been far less disruptive. GE's acquisitions in the past decade—companies such as Employers Reinsurance and Kidder, Peabody—have tended to be in areas like financial services where GE had already carved out niches. They were thus less disruptive to the organization as a whole. By alternating radical change with more organic modifications, Jack Welch has carefully buttressed the organization's stability, thereby making major changes more feasible. That's dynamic stability.

Dynamic Stability in Detail

At its essence, dynamic stability is a process of continual but relatively small change efforts that involve the reconfiguration of existing practices and business models rather than the creation of new ones. In addition to

tinkering and kludging, which differ from each other
mainly in scale, dynamic stability requires what I call
pacing—the big and small changes must be implemented at the right intervals. Let's look first at what I
mean by tinkering.

TINKERING

We all know a Mr. Fixit, someone who is always making
things, fiddling with odd nuts and bolts and pieces of old
washing machines. Similarly, some of the greatest
change masters—companies such as 3M and Hewlett-
Packard—are world-class tinkerers. They go into the corporate basement, so to speak, where they rapidly pull
together inspired solutions to their problems. Dow
Chemical, for example, developed Saran Wrap for an
industrial-coating application. With a little tinkering—
and a lot of expertise in marketing and branded consumer products—Dow successfully aimed the product at
consumers, an entirely different market.

Perhaps the most successful example of tinkering I
have witnessed was at a company that produces military
helicopters. The company's production runs had been
extremely small, typically just four helicopters. Each helicopter was customized for a specific type of mission—
submarine hunting, for example, or tank busting.
According to one engineer, no two helicopters came out
the same. Even identically designed helicopters required
a lot of jiggling to get all the parts working together. That
production style was fine as long as military budgets
were big, but the market became much more competitive
after the end of the cold war. The company was under
intense pressure to achieve economies of scale in development and production. It needed to change.

The organization itself, however, had little desire or energy to heed the call. It had a long history of big, expensive, failed changes, and employees were burned out and cynical. Desperate for a solution, managers discovered they already had a very good product-development model in the company's software division. They believed the model could be adapted to helicopter production to minimize product-design costs. Managers also realized they could improve production economics by using employees who already had experience with mass production in the auto industry. The company developed a new production strategy, which it called the Barbie doll. It built a base helicopter that could be dressed up with a set of accessories—guns, bombs, avionics—for customers in the military to play with. The strategy allowed the company to reap the benefits of both mass production and mass customization.

Nothing brand-new was created in this instance. The auto industry knowledge and the software development processes were already in place, as were the employees who made the change happen. The techniques are now well established in the company, and the not-invented-here syndrome is no longer an issue. Tinkering, of course, does not guarantee successful change. But it is less costly, less destabilizing, and quicker than creative destruction and invention.

KLUDGING

Kludging is tinkering, but with a college education. It takes place on a larger scale and involves many more parts. Some of the parts can come from outside a company's existing portfolio—as they do in mergers and acquisitions—but usually the components of a kludge are assets lying around an organization's backyard, such as skills in particular functions or standard technologies or models.

Because they are so large, kludges can result in the creation of a division or an entire business. Consider the case of GKN, a British industrial conglomerate. Starting in the early 1980s, contract cancellations started to pose a real problem. The organization would typically land contracts and then find engineers to staff the projects, but sometimes contracts would get postponed or canceled, leaving engineers idle.

To deal with this recurrent situation, GKN's units began to rent out their idle engineers for short assignments elsewhere, pulling them back into the organization as needed. The units started the practice on an informal basis, but it proved so successful that GKN created a new company to manage the hiring out of its own—and other companies'—engineers on short-term contracts. The new company, CEDU, is for all intents and purposes a sophisticated employment agency. The change in the status quo has been almost painless. The business model had been known in the organization for years. To make more money from it, all GKN had to do was formalize the practice in a new company.

Old-economy companies that try to adapt to the new economy can use kludging very effectively—they don't have to start Internet businesses from scratch. Consider Barnesandnoble.com. Dotcom, as it is known internally, saw that it could adapt Barnes & Noble's brands—along with its bricks-and-mortar capabilities in procuring books, paying publishers, and managing inventory— for e-commerce. As Dotcom CEO Stephen Riggio puts it, "It's all there. . . . As a result, our on-line company has been able to hit the ground running." To complete its

capabilities, Dotcom has borrowed resources from outside its boundaries: a suite of software acquired from
Firefly, an extensive list of potential customers from AOL,
and a pricing strategy copied from its key competitor,
Amazon. Little at Dotcom was invented from scratch.

PACING

Most proponents of change management argue that you
have to change as much as you can as quickly as you can
to stay ahead of the competition. That advice is not so
much wrong as overgeneralized. Like individuals, organizations have different needs for change. Organizations
that have consistently avoided change may need to
undergo rapid, destructive change. Companies that
already have been changing rapidly face a different
challenge—they must learn to shift down from highly
destabilizing and disruptive change to tinkering and
kludging.

One business leader who understands the value of
pacing is Lou Gerstner. At IBM and, before that, at
American Express Travel Related Services (TRS) and RJR
Nabisco, his initial impact was pure creative destruction.
In his first nine months at TRS, for example, Gerstner
launched a massive reorganization of the card and trav-
eler's check businesses, which was accompanied by a
widespread shift of managers across those units. A rash
of new product introductions followed quickly. TRS's
nine-month transformation was, in Gerstner's words,
like "breaking the four-minute mile."

But Gerstner had a genius for knowing when it was
time to rest. He was alert to early signs of change fatigue:
cynicism and burnout. He recognized that the success of
his overall change campaign depended on the stability of

the units involved, and he was very thoughtful about how and when to intersperse the small changes among the big. At TRS, no new products were launched and no new executives were brought in from outside for 18 months after Gerstner's initial blitz. But he didn't sit back and do nothing. He tinkered constantly to prevent the company from drifting into inertia; he played with the structure, with the compensation system, with TRS product offerings. But the unthreatening nature of the interim changes allowed the company to better absorb a second wave of product launches and restructurings when it came.

Incidentally, it's particularly easy for companies in the hurly-burly of the new economy to forget the importance of slowing down. But being first does not necessarily mean being fastest. Remember the old story of the two unfortunate campers in the jungle who noticed a jaguar stalking them. One of them sat down and put on his running shoes. The other looked at him incredulously. "You're crazy," he said. "You're never going to outrun that jaguar." "I don't need to," the first replied. "I only need to outrun you."

Four Operating Guidelines

Like many managerial practices, dynamic stability is as much an art as a science. But according to my research, the companies that successfully tinker and kludge use four operating guidelines. They are as follows:

Reward Shameless Borrowing. The first rule of dynamic stability is that companies must be willing to noodle with what already exists—and invent from scratch only as a last resort. Following such a rule isn't easy. In U.S.

culture, imitation is a sign of weakness, if not moral turpitude. Imitators are seen as people who aren't smart enough to invent good ideas for themselves. But words like "copycat" and "impersonator" should be compliments, not insults. Companies need cultures that value creative imitation and condemn invention that is wasteful.

The glorification of invention leads companies to squander precious resources. The most egregious example of such a culture is probably the old General Motors. Because of its admiration for new inventions and its history of keeping brands separate, GM kept right on reinventing the wheel, sometimes quite literally. As a result, despite tremendous human and financial resources, GM has never been world-class in the efficiency of its product development.

Booz-Allen & Hamilton, the management consulting firm, had a similar problem. It used to lock up its expertise in "knowledge pyramids," each of which was carefully guarded by a partner at the top and a set of associates below. When a change in approach was needed to better serve a client, people in the pyramid laboriously reinvented strategies that probably could have been found in dozens of other such pyramids. Booz-Allen is a very different company today, however. With great success, it uses sophisticated knowledge management systems to capture, share, imitate—basically, tinker with—existing expertise, rather than reinvent it. Its culture generously rewards—or should I say mandates—imitation.

Of course, by shameless, I don't mean slavish; there's little value in applying an idea in a cookie-cutter fashion. Booz-Allen excels at creative imitation: the best elements of an idea, process, or structure are reconfigured and customized to serve each client's needs.

Appoint a Chief Memory Officer. Only by remembering the past as we tinker and kludge can we avoid making the same old mistakes—and take advantage of valuable opportunities.

Apple has successfully resurrected the past with the iMac, which harks back to the groundbreaking Apple II and Macintosh. Apple has recreated a culture that challenges employees to build something "insanely great"—in this case an affordable computer with a distinctive look. There is nothing essentially new about this mix—it's just that the company had forgotten its past as it ran through four CEOs in as many years. The return of Steve Jobs made the renaissance possible.

Jobs serves a dual function at Apple. He not only provides charismatic leadership, he also serves as the organization's memory—which as founder he is well placed to do. Some companies hire historians to write their histories; others remember the simple truth that their long-tenured employees are their best historians. These "chief memory officers" are informally asked to review past projects, successful and unsuccessful, before any "innovation" is launched—or relaunched. Every company needs memory keepers with the clout to make themselves heard. They help the organization undertake change without engendering unnecessary chaos, cynicism, or burnout.

By contrast, companies that forget the past are condemned to relive it—often endangering dynamic stability. Citicorp's regional organizational structure repeatedly alternates between combining sales and operations and keeping them separate. From time to time the company tries to integrate sales and operations by placing them under one roof, only to discover that sales isn't getting the attention it needs in the highly competitive

financial services industry. So Citicorp separates them
again. The alternations take place unpredictably across
many regional operations, and the waste of resources
is colossal.

Tinker and Kludge Internally First. Dynamic stability is
much easier to manage if you stay inside the organization. Just as the body is more likely to reject a foreign
organ than its own, an organization has greater difficulty
reconfiguring imported parts. Consider quality circles:
some 90% of *Fortune* 500 companies borrowed this tool
from Japanese manufacturers in the 1970s and early
1980s. By 1982, 80% had rejected it. Companies would
have been better off tinkering with teams, participative-
management approaches, and quality processes existing
in-house before trying to import a management technique developed halfway around the world in an
extremely different culture.

Kludging by using external parts is even more
difficult than tinkering, as the 70% failure rate of
acquisitions suggests. That's why many of the companies that have grown most successfully have done so
organically. Southwest Airlines has become one of the
country's largest airlines through a series of internal
kludges. Unlike its competitors, Southwest replicates
parts of its existing business formula, such as its
human-resource management practices, in new re-
gions, so that other mini-airlines are created and added
to the portfolio.

Sometimes companies can't avoid going outside—to
get a technology that doesn't exist in-house, for example.
But the company has to know which organizations it can
and can't acquire. Cisco Systems, an adept external
kludger, will consider a company for acquisition only if it

is small and shows strong growth prospects; the target company also has to be located near a Cisco R&D center and must have a culture that's compatible with Cisco's. As a result, Cisco retains 90% of the employees who join through acquisition—and by retaining those employees, it retains the knowledge and skills that attracted Cisco to the acquisition target in the first place.

Hire Generalists. A company dedicated to dynamic stability needs generalists. Generalists are often derided as jacks-of-all-trades and masters of none. But their range of skills lets them combine disparate ideas, techniques, processes, and cultures. In other words, they can tinker and kludge. What's more, generalists are typically more open-minded and less biased than specialists are. They like to get their hands dirty. They also like to job hop. Take Marty Homlish, one of the key architects of the Sony PlayStation. As Homlish moved from position to position, he acquired a powerful mix of eclectic skills. Each new turnaround he masterminded gave him an opportunity to add to his already extensive bag of tricks. People like Homlish make it possible to change without pain; they are an essential ingredient of dynamic stability.

How do you know who the generalists are? Kludgers and tinkerers are boundary spanners. They don't eat lunch with the same coworkers every day. Their friends are not clones of one another, sharing the same perspectives on life. Their friends are rock musicians, plumbers, nuclear physicists. They travel a lot and not in tour buses. They like to try different things and are easily bored. Generalists have a broad array of ideas and techniques. As a result, they have at their fingertips the raw materials for tinkering, kludging, and sustaining dynamic stability.

CHANGE HAS BEEN WITH US FOREVER, and it always will be, but the idea of change itself is changing. Companies are increasingly aware of the need to combat chaos, cynicism, and burnout by using change tools that are less disruptive. Oscillation between big changes and small changes helps ensure dynamic stability in organizations. More critically, it paves the way for change that succeeds.

Originally published in July–August 2000
Reprint R00040I

The Hard Side of
Change Management

HAROLD L. SIRKIN, PERRY KEENAN,
AND ALAN JACKSON

Executive Summary

EVERYONE AGREES THAT managing change is
tough, but few can agree on how to do it. Most experts
are obsessed with "soft" issues, such as culture and motivation, but, say the authors, focusing on these issues
alone won't bring about change. Companies also need
to consider the hard factors—like the time it takes to complete a change initiative, the number of people required
to execute it, and so forth.

When the authors studied change initiatives at 225
companies, they found a consistent correlation between
the outcomes of change programs (success versus failure) and four hard factors, which they called DICE: project *duration*, particularly the time between project
reviews; *integrity of performance*, or the capabilities of
project teams; the level of *commitment* of senior executives and staff; and the additional *effort* required of

employees directly affected by the change. The DICE framework is a simple formula for calculating how well a company is implementing, or will be able to implement, its change initiatives. The framework comprises a set of simple questions that help executives score their projects on each of the four factors; the lower the score, the more likely the project will succeed. Companies can use DICE assessments to force conversations about projects, to gauge whether projects are on track or in trouble, and to manage project portfolios.

The authors have used these four factors to predict the outcomes and guide the execution of more than 1,000 change management programs worldwide. Not only has the correlation held, but no other factors (or combination of factors) have predicted outcomes as successfully.

WHEN FRENCH NOVELIST Jean-Baptiste Alphonse Karr wrote "Plus ça change, plus c'est la même chose," he could have been penning an epigram about change management. For over three decades, academics, managers, and consultants, realizing that transforming organizations is difficult, have dissected the subject. They've sung the praises of leaders who communicate vision and walk the talk in order to make change efforts succeed. They've sanctified the importance of changing organizational culture and employees' attitudes. They've teased out the tensions between top-down transformation efforts and participatory approaches to change. And they've exhorted companies to launch campaigns that appeal to people's hearts and minds. Still, studies show that in most organizations, two out of three transformation initiatives fail. The more things change, the more they stay the same.

Managing change *is* tough, but part of the problem is that there is little agreement on what factors most influence transformation initiatives. Ask five executives to name the one factor critical for the success of these programs, and you'll probably get five different answers. That's because each manager looks at an initiative from his or her viewpoint and, based on personal experience, focuses on different success factors. The experts, too, offer different perspectives. A recent search on Amazon.com for books on "change and management" turned up 6,153 titles, each with a distinct take on the topic. Those ideas have a lot to offer, but taken together, they force companies to tackle many priorities simultaneously, which spreads resources and skills thin. Moreover, executives use different approaches in different parts of the organization, which compounds the turmoil that usually accompanies change.

In recent years, many change management gurus have focused on soft issues, such as culture, leadership, and motivation. Such elements are important for success, but managing these aspects alone isn't sufficient to implement transformation projects. Soft factors don't directly influence the outcomes of many change programs. For instance, visionary leadership is often vital for transformation projects, but not always. The same can be said about communication with employees. Moreover, it isn't easy to change attitudes or relationships; they're deeply ingrained in organizations and people. And although changes in, say, culture or motivation levels can be indirectly gauged through surveys and interviews, it's tough to get reliable data on soft factors.

What's missing, we believe, is a focus on the not-so-fashionable aspects of change management: the hard factors. These factors bear three distinct characteristics. First, companies are able to measure them in direct or indirect ways. Second, companies can easily communicate their importance, both within and outside organizations. Third, and perhaps most important, businesses are capable of influencing those elements quickly. Some of the hard factors that affect a transformation initiative are the time necessary to complete it, the number of people required to execute it, and the financial results that intended actions are expected to achieve. Our research shows that change projects fail to get off the ground when companies neglect the hard factors. That doesn't mean that executives can ignore the soft elements; that would be a grave mistake. However, if companies don't pay attention to the hard issues first, transformation programs will break down before the soft elements come into play.

That's a lesson we learned when we identified the common denominators of change. In 1992, we started with the contrarian hypothesis that organizations handle transformations in remarkably similar ways. We researched projects in a number of industries and countries to identify those common elements. Our initial 225-company study revealed a consistent correlation between the outcomes (success or failure) of change programs and four hard factors: project *duration,* particularly the time between project reviews; performance *integrity,* or the capabilities of project teams; the *commitment* of both senior executives and the staff whom the change will affect the most; and the additional *effort* that employees must make to cope with the change. We called these variables the DICE factors because we could load them in favor of projects' success.

We completed our study in 1994, and in the 11 years since then, the Boston Consulting Group has used those four factors to predict the outcomes, and guide the execution, of more than 1,000 change management initiatives worldwide. Not only has the correlation held, but no other factors (or combination of factors) have predicted outcomes as well.

The Four Key Factors

If you think about it, the different ways in which organizations combine the four factors create a continuum—from projects that are set up to succeed to those that are set up to fail. At one extreme, a short project led by a skilled, motivated, and cohesive team, championed by top management and implemented in a department that is receptive to the change and has to put in very little additional effort, is bound to succeed. At the other extreme, a long, drawn-out project executed by an inexpert, unenthusiastic, and disjointed team, without any top-level sponsors and targeted at a function that dislikes the change and has to do a lot of extra work, will fail. Businesses can easily identify change programs at either end of the spectrum, but most initiatives occupy the middle ground where the likelihood of success or failure is difficult to assess. Executives must study the four DICE factors carefully to figure out if their change programs will fly—or die.

DURATION

Companies make the mistake of worrying mostly about the time it will take to implement change programs. They assume that the longer an initiative carries on, the more likely it is to fail—the early impetus will peter out, windows of opportunity will close, objectives will be forgotten, key supporters will leave or lose their enthusiasm, and problems will accumulate. However, contrary to popular perception, our studies show that a long project that is reviewed frequently is more likely to succeed than a short project that isn't reviewed frequently. Thus, the time between reviews is more critical for success than a project's life span.

Companies should formally review transformation projects at least bimonthly since, in our experience, the probability that change initiatives will run into trouble rises exponentially when the time between reviews exceeds eight weeks. Whether reviews should be scheduled even more frequently depends on how long executives feel the project can carry on without going off track. Complex projects should be reviewed fortnightly; more familiar or straightforward initiatives can be assessed every six to eight weeks.

Scheduling milestones and assessing their impact are the best way by which executives can review the execution of projects, identify gaps, and spot new risks. The most effective milestones are those that describe major actions or achievements rather than day-to-day activities. They must enable senior executives and project sponsors to confirm that the project has made progress since the last review took place. Good milestones encompass a number of tasks that teams must complete. For example, describing a particular milestone as "Consultations with Stakeholders Completed" is more effective than "Consult Stakeholders" because it represents an achievement and shows that the project has made headway. Moreover, it suggests that several activities were completed—identifying stakeholders, assessing their needs, and talking to them about the project. When a milestone looks as though it won't be reached on time, the project team must try to understand why, take corrective actions, and learn from the experience to prevent problems from recurring.

Review of such a milestone—what we refer to as a "learning milestone"—isn't an impromptu assessment of the Monday-morning kind. It should be a formal occasion during which senior-management sponsors and the project team evaluate the latter's performance on all the dimensions that have a bearing on success and failure. The team must provide a concise report of its progress, and members and sponsors must check if the team is on track to complete, or has finished all the tasks to deliver, the milestone. They should also determine whether achieving the milestone has had the desired effect on the company; discuss the problems the team faced in reaching the milestone; and determine how that accomplishment will affect the next phase of the project. Sponsors and team members must have the power to address weaknesses. When necessary, they should alter processes, agree to push for more or different resources, or suggest a new direction. At these meetings, senior executives must pay special attention to the dynamics within teams, changes in the organization's perceptions about the initiative, and communications from the top.

INTEGRITY

By performance integrity, we mean the extent to which companies can rely on teams of managers, supervisors, and staff to execute change projects successfully. In a perfect world, every team would be flawless, but no business has enough great people to ensure that. Besides, senior executives are often reluctant to allow star performers to join change efforts because regular work can suffer. But since the success of change programs depends on the quality of teams, companies must free up the best staff while making sure that day-to-day operations don't falter. In companies that have succeeded in implementing change programs, we find that employees go the extra mile to ensure their day-to-day work gets done.

Since project teams handle a wide range of activities, resources, pressures, external stimuli, and unforeseen obstacles, they must be cohesive and well led. It's not enough for senior executives to ask people at the watercooler if a project team is doing well; they must clarify members' roles, commitments, and accountability. They must choose the team leader and, most important, work out the team's composition.

Smart executive sponsors, we find, are very inclusive when picking teams. They identify talent by soliciting names from key colleagues, including human resource managers; by circulating criteria they have drawn up; and by looking for top performers in all functions. While they accept volunteers, they take care not to choose only supporters of the change initiative. Senior executives personally interview people so that they can construct the right portfolio of skills, knowledge, and social networks. They also decide if potential team members should commit all their time to the project; if not, they must ask them to allocate specific days or times of the day to the initiative. Top management makes public the parameters on which it will judge the team's performance and how that evaluation fits into the company's regular appraisal process. Once the project gets under way, sponsors must measure the cohesion of teams by administering confidential surveys to solicit members' opinions.

Executives often make the mistake of assuming that because someone is a good, well-liked manager, he or she will also make a decent team leader. That sounds reasonable, but effective managers of the status quo aren't necessarily good at changing organizations. Usually, good team leaders have problem-solving skills, are results oriented, are methodical in their approach but tolerate ambiguity, are organizationally savvy, are willing to accept responsibility for decisions, and while being highly motivated, don't crave the limelight. A CEO who successfully led two major transformation projects in the past ten years used these six criteria to quiz senior executives about the caliber of nominees for project teams. The top management team rejected one in three candidates, on average, before finalizing the teams.

COMMITMENT

Companies must boost the commitment of two different groups of people if they want change projects to take root: They must get visible backing from the most influential executives (what we call C1), who are not necessarily those with the top titles. And they must take into account the enthusiasm—or often, lack thereof—of the people who must deal with the new systems, processes, or ways of working (C2).

Top-level commitment is vital to engendering commitment from those at the coal face. If employees don't see that the company's leadership is backing a project, they're unlikely to change. No amount of top-level support is too much. In 1999, when we were working with the CEO of a consumer products company, he told us that he was doing much more than necessary to display his support for a nettlesome project. When we talked to line managers, they said that the CEO had extended very little backing for the project. They felt that if he wanted the project to succeed, he would have to support it more visibly! A rule of thumb: When you feel that you are talking up a change initiative at least three times more than you need to, your managers will feel that you are backing the transformation.

Sometimes, senior executives are reluctant to back initiatives. That's understandable; they're often bringing about changes that may negatively affect employees' jobs and lives. However, if senior executives do not communicate the need for change, and what it means for employees, they endanger their projects' success. In one financial services firm, top management's commitment to a program that would improve cycle times, reduce errors, and slash costs was low because it entailed layoffs. Senior executives found it gut-wrenching to talk about layoffs in an organization that had prided itself on being a place where good people could find lifetime employment. However, the CEO realized that he needed to tackle the thorny issues around the layoffs to get the project implemented on schedule. He tapped a senior company veteran to organize a series of speeches and meetings in order to provide consistent explanations for the layoffs, the timing, the consequences for job security, and so on. He also appointed a well-respected general manager to lead the change program. Those actions reassured employees that the organization would tackle the layoffs in a professional and humane fashion.

Companies often underestimate the role that managers and staff play in transformation efforts. By communicating with them too late or inconsistently, senior executives end up alienating the people who are most affected by the changes. It's surprising how often something senior executives believe is a good thing is seen by staff as a bad thing, or a message that senior executives think is perfectly clear is misunderstood. That usually happens when senior executives articulate subtly different versions of critical messages. For instance, in one company that applied the DICE framework, scores for a project showed a low degree of staff commitment. It turned out that these employees had become confused, even distrustful, because one senior manager had said, "Layoffs will not occur," while another had said, "They are not expected to occur."

Organizations also underestimate their ability to build staff support. A simple effort to reach out to employees can turn them into champions of new ideas. For example, in the 1990s, a major American energy producer was unable to get the support of mid-level managers, supervisors, and workers for a productivity improvement program. After trying several times, the company's senior executives decided to hold a series of one-on-one conversations with mid-level managers in a last-ditch effort to win them over. The conversations focused on the program's objectives, its impact on employees, and why the organization might not be able to survive without the changes. Partly because of the straight talk, the initiative gained some momentum. This allowed a project team to demonstrate a series of quick wins, which gave the initiative a new lease on life.

EFFORT

When companies launch transformation efforts, they frequently don't realize, or know how to deal with the fact, that employees are already busy with their day-to-day responsibilities. According to staffing tables, people in many businesses work 80-plus-hour weeks. If, on top of existing responsibilities, line managers and staff have to deal with changes to their work or to the systems they use, they will resist.

Project teams must calculate how much work employees will have to do beyond their existing responsibilities to change over to new processes. Ideally, no one's workload should increase more than 10%. Go beyond that, and the initiative will probably run into trouble. Resources will become overstretched and compromise either the change program or normal operations. Employee morale will fall, and conflict may arise between teams and line staff. To minimize the dangers, project managers should use a simple metric like the percentage increase in effort the employees who must cope with the new ways feel they must contribute. They should also check if the additional effort they have demanded comes on top of heavy workloads and if employees are likely to resist the project because it will demand more of their scarce time.

Companies must decide whether to take away some of the regular work of employees who will play key roles in the transformation project. Companies can start by ridding these employees of discretionary or nonessential responsibilities. In addition, firms should review all the other projects in the operating plan and assess which ones are critical for the change effort. At one company, the project steering committee delayed or restructured 120 out of 250 subprojects so that some line managers could focus on top-priority projects. Another way to relieve pressure is for the company to bring in temporary workers, like retired managers, to carry out routine activities or to outsource current processes until the changeover is complete. Handing off routine work or delaying projects is costly and time-consuming, so companies need to think through such issues before kicking off transformation efforts.

Creating the Framework

As we came to understand the four factors better, we created a framework that would help executives evaluate their transformation initiatives and shine a spotlight on interventions that would improve their chances of success. We developed a scoring system based on the variables that affect each factor. Executives can assign scores to the DICE factors and combine them to arrive at a project score. (See the exhibit "Calculating DICE Scores.")

Although the assessments are subjective, the system gives companies an objective framework for making those decisions. Moreover, the scoring mechanism ensures that executives are evaluating projects and making trade-offs more consistently across projects.

A company can compare its DICE score on the day it kicks off a project with the scores of previous projects, as well as their outcomes, to check if the initiative has been set up for success. When we calculated the scores of the 225 change projects in our database and compared them with the outcomes, the analysis was compelling. Projects clearly fell into three categories, or zones: *Win,* which means that any project with a score in that range is statistically likely to succeed; *worry,* which suggests that the project's outcome is hard to predict; and *woe,* which implies that the project is totally unpredictable or fated for mediocrity or failure. (See the exhibit "DICE Scores Predict Project Outcomes.")

Companies can track how change projects are faring by calculating scores over time or before and after they have made changes to a project's structure. The four

Calculating DICE Scores

Companies can determine if their change programs will succeed by asking executives to calculate scores for each of the four factors of the DICE framework—duration, integrity, commitment, and effort. They must grade each factor on a scale from 1 to 4 (using fractions, if necessary); the lower the score, the better. Thus, a score of 1 suggests that the factor is highly likely to contribute to success, and a score of 4 means that it is highly unlikely to contribute to success. We find that the following questions and scoring guidelines allow executives to rate transformation initiatives effectively:

Duration [D]

Ask: Do formal project reviews occur regularly? If the project will take more than two months to complete, what is the average time between reviews?

Score: If the time between project reviews is less than two months, you should give the project 1 point. If the time is between two and four months, you should award the project 2 points; between four and eight months, 3 points; and if reviews are more than eight months apart, give the project 4 points.

Integrity of Performance [I]

Ask: Is the team leader capable? How strong are team members' skills and motivations? Do they have sufficient time to spend on the change initiative?

Score: If the project team is led by a highly capable leader who is respected by peers, if the members have the skills and motivation to complete the project in the stipulated time frame, and if the company has assigned at least 50% of the team members' time to the project, you can give the project 1 point. If the team is lacking on all those dimensions, you should award the project 4 points. If the team's capabilities are somewhere in between, assign the project 2 or 3 points.

Senior Management Commitment [C₁]

Ask: Do senior executives regularly communicate the reason for the change and the importance of its success? Is the message convincing? Is the message consistent, both across the top management team and over time? Has top management devoted enough resources to the change program?

Score: If senior management has, through actions and words, clearly communicated the need for change, you must give the project 1 point. If senior executives appear to be neutral, it gets 2 or 3 points. If managers perceive senior executives to be reluctant to support the change, award the project 4 points.

Local-Level Commitment [C₂]

Ask: Do the employees most affected by the change understand the reason for it and believe it's worthwhile? Are they enthusiastic and supportive or worried and obstructive?

Score: If employees are eager to take on the change initiative, you can give the project 1 point, and if they are just willing, 2 points. If they're reluctant or strongly reluctant, you should award the project 3 or 4 points.

Effort [E]

Ask: What is the percentage of increased effort that employees must make to implement the change effort? Does the incremental effort come on top of a heavy workload? Have people strongly resisted the increased demands on them?

Score: If the project requires less than 10% extra work by employees, you can give it 1 point. If it's 10% to 20% extra, it should get 2 points. If it's 20% to 40%, it must be 3 points. And if it's more than 40% additional work, you should give the project 4 points.

Executives can combine the four elements into a project score. When we conducted a regression analysis of our database of change efforts, we found that the combination that correlates most closely with actual outcomes doubles the weight given to team performance (1) and senior management commitment (C_1). That translates into the following formula:

DICE Score = $D + (2 \times I) + (2 \times C_1) + C_2 + E$

In the 1-to-4 scoring system, the formula generates overall scores that range from 7 to 28. Companies can compare a project's score with those of past projects and their outcomes to assess if the project is slated for success or failure. Our data show a clear distribution of scores:

Scores between 7 and 14: The project is very likely to succeed. We call this the Win Zone.

Scores higher than 14 but lower than 17: Risks to the project's success are rising, particularly as the score approaches 17. This is the Worry Zone.

Scores over 17: The project is extremely risky. If a project scores over 17 and under 19 points, the risks to success are very high. Beyond 19, the project is unlikely to succeed. That's why we call this the Woe Zone.

We have changed the boundaries of the zones over time. For instance, the Worry Zone was between 14 and 21 points at first, and the Woe Zone from 21 to 28 points. But we found that companies prefer to be alerted to trouble as soon as outcomes become unpredictable (17 to 20 points). We therefore compressed the Worry Zone and expanded the Woe Zone.

(continued)

Calculating DICE Scores (continued)

[D]	[I]	[C₁]	[C₂]	[E]

Calculate ⟹ Dice Score = $D + 2I + 2C_1 + C_2 + E$ ⟹ [ ] Plot

Likely Outcome — Highly Successful ⟺ Highly Unsuccessful

Win   Worry   Woe

DICE Score: 7 8 9 10 11 12 13 14 15 16 17 18 19 20 21 22 23 24 25 26 27 28 factors offer a litmus test that executives can use to assess the probability of success for a given project or set of projects. Consider the case of a large Australian bank that in 1994 wanted to restructure its back-office operations. Senior executives agreed on the rationale for the change but differed on whether the bank could achieve its objectives, since the transformation required major changes in processes and organizational structures. Bringing the team and the senior executives together long enough to sort out their differences proved impossible; people were just too busy. That's when the project team decided to analyze the initiative using the DICE framework.

Doing so condensed what could have been a free-flowing two-day debate into a sharp two-hour discussion. The focus on just four elements generated a clear picture of the project's strengths and weaknesses. For instance, managers learned that the restructuring would take eight months to implement but that it had poorly defined milestones and reviews. Although the project team was capable and senior management showed reasonable commitment to the effort, there was room for improvement in both areas. The back-office workforce was hostile to the proposed changes since more than 20% of these people would lose their jobs. Managers and employees agreed that the back-office staff would need to muster 10% to 20% more effort on top of its existing commitments during the implementation. On the DICE scale, the project was deep in the Woe Zone.

However, the assessment also led managers to take steps to increase the possibility of success before they started the project. The bank decided to split the project time line into two—one short-term and one long-term. Doing so allowed the bank to schedule review points more frequently and to maximize team members' ability to learn from experience before the transformation grew in complexity. To improve staff commitment, the bank decided to devote more time to explaining why the change was necessary and how the institution would support the staff during the implementation. The bank also took a closer look at the people who would be involved in the project and changed some of the team leaders when it realized that they lacked the necessary skills. Finally, senior managers made a concerted effort to show their

---

DICE Scores Predict Project Outcomes

When we plotted the DICE scores of 225 change management initiatives on the horizontal axis, and the outcomes of those projects on the vertical axis, we found three sets of correlations. Projects with DICE scores between 7 and 14 were usually successful; those with scores over 14 and under 17 were unpredictable; and projects with scores over 17 were usually unsuccessful. We named the three zones Win, Worry, and Woe, respectively. (Each number plotted on the graph represents the number of projects, out of the 225 projects, having a particular DICE score.)

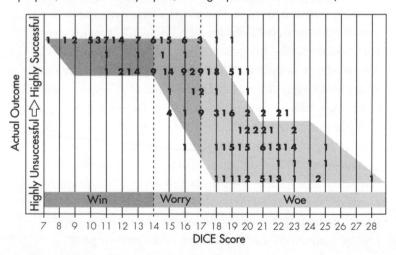

backing for the initiative by holding a traveling road show to explain the project to people at all levels of the organization. Taken together, the bank's actions and plans shifted the project into the Win Zone. Fourteen months later, the bank completed the project—on time and below budget.

Applying the DICE Framework

The simplicity of the DICE framework often proves to be its biggest problem; executives seem to desire more complex answers. By overlooking the obvious, however, they often end up making compromises that don't work. Smart companies try to ensure that they don't fall into that trap by using the DICE framework in one of three ways.

TRACK PROJECTS

Some companies train managers in how to use the DICE framework before they start transformation programs. Executives use spreadsheet-based versions of the tool to calculate the DICE scores of the various components of the program and to compare them with past scores. Over time, every score must be balanced against the trajectory of scores and, as we shall see next, the portfolio of scores.

Senior executives often use DICE assessments as early warning indicators that transformation initiatives are in trouble. That's how Amgen, the $10.6 billion biotechnology company, used the DICE framework. In 2001, the company realigned its operations around some key processes, broadened its offerings, relaunched some mature products, allied with some firms and acquired others, and launched several innovations. To avoid implementation problems, Amgen's top management team used the DICE framework to gauge how effectively it had allocated people, senior management time, and other resources. As soon as projects reported troubling scores, designated executives paid attention to them. They reviewed the projects more often, reconfigured the teams, and allocated more resources to them. In one area of the change project, Amgen used DICE to track 300 initiatives and reconfigured 200 of them.

Both big and small organizations can put the tool to good use. Take the case of a hospital that kicked off six change projects in the late 1990s. Each initiative involved a lot of investment, had significant clinical implications, or both. The hospital's general manager felt that some projects were going well but was concerned about others. He wasn't able to attribute his concerns to anything other than a bad feeling. However, when the general manager used the DICE framework, he was able to confirm his suspicions. After a 45-minute discussion with project managers and other key people, he established that three projects were in the Win Zone but two were in the Woe Zone and one was in the Worry Zone.

The strongest projects, the general manager found, consumed more than their fair share of resources. Senior hospital staff sensed that those projects would succeed and spent more time promoting them, attending meetings about them, and making sure they had sufficient resources. By contrast, no one enjoyed attending meetings on projects that were performing poorly. So the general manager stopped attending meetings for the projects that were on track; he attended only sessions that related to the three underperforming ones. He pulled some managers from the projects that were progressing smoothly and moved them to the riskier efforts. He added more milestones to the struggling enterprises, delayed their completion, and pushed hard for improvement. Those steps helped ensure that all six projects met their objectives.

MANAGE PORTFOLIOS OF PROJECTS

When companies launch large transformation programs, they kick off many projects to attain their objectives. But if executives don't manage the portfolio properly, those tasks end up competing for attention and resources. For instance, senior executives may choose the best employees for projects they have sponsored or lavish attention on pet projects rather than on those that need attention. By deploying our framework before they start transformation initiatives, companies can identify problem projects in portfolios, focus execution expertise and senior management attention where it is most needed, and defuse political issues.

Take, for example, the case of an Australasian manufacturing company that had planned a set of 40 projects as part of a program to improve profitability. Since some had greater financial implications than others, the company's general manager called for a meeting with all the project owners and senior managers. The group went through each project, debating its DICE score and identifying the problem areas. After listing all the scores and issues, the general manager walked to a whiteboard and circled the five most important projects. "I'm prepared to accept that some projects will start off in the Worry Zone, though I won't accept anything outside the middle of this zone for more than a few weeks. For the top five, we're not going to start until these are well within the

Win Zone. What do we have to do to achieve that?" he asked.

The group began thinking and acting right away. It moved people around on teams, reconfigured some projects, and identified those that senior managers should pay more attention to—all of which helped raise DICE scores before implementation began. The most important projects were set up for resounding success while most of the remaining ones managed to get into the Win Zone. The group left some projects in the Worry Zone, but it agreed to track them closely to ensure that their scores improved. In our experience, that's the right thing to do. When companies are trying to overhaul themselves, they shouldn't have all their projects in the Win Zone; if they do, they are not ambitious enough. Transformations should entail fundamental changes that stretch an organization.

●

FORCE CONVERSATION

When different executives calculate DICE scores for the same project, the results can vary widely. The difference in scores is particularly important in terms of the dialogue it triggers. It provokes participants and engages them in debate over questions like "Why do we see the project in these different ways?" and "What can we agree to do to ensure that the project will succeed?" That's critical, because even people within the same organization lack a common framework for discussing problems with change initiatives. Prejudices, differences in perspectives, and a reluctance or inability to speak up can block effective debates. By using the DICE framework, companies can create a common language and force the right discussions.

Sometimes, companies hold workshops to review floundering projects. At those two- to four-hour sessions, groups of eight to 15 senior and middle managers, along with the project team and the project sponsors, hold a candid dialogue. The debate usually moves beyond the project's scores to the underlying causes of problems and possible remedies. The workshops bring diverse opinions to light, which often can be combined into innovative solutions. Consider, for example, the manner in which DICE workshops helped a telecommunications service provider that had planned a major transformation effort. Consisting of five strategic initiatives and 50 subprojects that needed to be up and running quickly, the program confronted some serious obstacles. The projects' goals, time lines, and revenue objectives were unclear. There were delays in approving business cases, a dearth of rigor and focus in planning and identifying milestones, and a shortage of resources. There were leadership issues, too. For example, executive-level shortcomings had resulted in poor coordination of projects and a misjudgment of risks.

To put the transformation program on track, the telecom company incorporated DICE into project managers' tool kits. The Project Management Office arranged a series of workshops to analyze issues and decide future steps. One workshop, for example, was devoted to three new product development projects, two of which had landed in the Woe Zone and one in the Worry Zone. Participants traced the problems to tension between managers and technology experts, underfunding, lack of manpower, and poor definition of the projects' scopes. They eventually agreed on three remedial actions: holding a conflict-resolution meeting between the directors in charge of technology and those responsible for the core business; making sure senior leadership paid immediate attention to the resource issues; and bringing together the project team and the line-of-business head to formalize project objectives. With the project sponsor committed to those actions, the three projects had improved their DICE scores and thus their chances of success at the time this article went to press.

Conversations about DICE scores are particularly useful for large-scale transformations that cut across business units, functions, and locations. In such change efforts, it is critical to find the right balance between centralized oversight, which ensures that everyone in the organization takes the effort seriously and understands the goals, and the autonomy that various initiatives need. Teams must have the flexibility and incentive to produce customized solutions for their markets, functions, and competitive environments. The balance is difficult to achieve without an explicit consideration of the DICE variables.

Take the case of a leading global beverage company that needed to increase operational efficiency and focus on the most promising brands and markets. The company also sought to make key processes such as consumer demand development and customer fulfillment more innovative. The CEO's goals were ambitious and required investing significant resources across the company. Top management faced enormous challenges in structuring the effort and in spawning projects that focused on the right issues. Executives knew that this was a multiyear effort, yet without tight schedules and oversight of individual projects, there was a risk that projects would take far too long to be completed and the results would taper off.

To mitigate the risks, senior managers decided to analyze each project at several levels of the organization. Using the DICE framework, they reviewed each effort every month until they felt confident that it was on track. After that, reviews occurred when projects met major milestones. No more than two months elapsed between reviews, even in the later stages of the program. The time between reviews at the project-team level was even shorter: Team leaders reviewed progress biweekly throughout the transformation. Some of the best people joined the effort full time. The human resources department took an active role in recruiting team members, thereby creating a virtuous cycle in which the best people began to seek involvement in various initiatives. During the course of the transformation, the company promoted several team members to line- and functional leadership positions because of their performance.

The company's change program resulted in hundreds of millions of dollars of value creation. Its once-stagnant brands began to grow, it cracked open new markets such as China, and sales and promotion activities were aligned with the fastest-growing channels. There were many moments during the process when inertia in the organization threatened to derail the change efforts. However, senior management's belief in focusing on the four key variables helped move the company to a higher trajectory of performance.

By providing a common language for change, the DICE framework allows companies to tap into the insight and experience of their employees. A great deal has been said about middle managers who want to block change. We find that most middle managers are prepared to support change efforts even if doing so involves additional work and uncertainty and puts their jobs at risk. However, they resist change because they don't have sufficient input in shaping those initiatives. Too often, they lack the tools, the language, and the forums in which to express legitimate concerns about the design and implementation of change projects. That's where a standard, quantitative, and simple framework comes in. By enabling frank conversations at all levels within organizations, the DICE framework helps people do the right thing by change.

The Four Factors

THESE FACTORS DETERMINE the outcome of any transformation initiative.

- **D.** The **duration** of time until the change program is completed if it has a short life span; if not short, the amount of time between reviews of milestones.

- **I.** The project team's performance **integrity;** that is, its ability to complete the initiative on time. That depends on members' skills and traits relative to the project's requirements.

- **C.** The **commitment** to change that top management (C1) and employees affected by the change (C2) display.

- **E.** The **effort** over and above the usual work that the change initiative demands of employees.

Originally published in October 2005
Reprint R0510G

About the Contributors

ERIC ABRAHAMSON is a management professor at Columbia Business School in New York City, where he teaches and carries out research on organizational behavior and change management.

RAM CHARAN was formerly on the faculties of Harvard Business School and Northwestern's Kellogg School. He is the author of numerous books.

DAVID A. GARVIN is the C. Roland Christensen Professor of Business Administration at Harvard Business School in Boston.

ALAN JACKSON is a Boston Consulting Group senior vice president in Sydney, Australia.

PERRY KEENAN is a Boston Consulting Group vice president and the global topic leader for rigorous program management based in Auckland, New Zealand.

W. CHAN KIM is the Boston Consulting Group Bruce D. Henderson Chair Professor of Strategy and International Management at Insead in Fontainebleau, France.

JOHN P. KOTTER is the Konosuke Matsushita Professor of Leadership (retired) at Harvard Business School in Boston.

RENÉE MAUBORGNE is the Insead Distinguished Fellow and a professor of strategy and management at Insead in Fontainebleau, France.

ROBERT E. QUINN is the Margaret Elliot Tracy Collegiate Professor of Business Administration in the organization and management group at the University of Michigan's Ross School of Business.

MICHAEL A. ROBERTO is an assistant professor of business administration at Harvard Business School

HAROLD L. SIRKIN is a Chicago-based senior vice president and the global operations practice leader of the Boston Consulting Group.

PAUL STREBEL is a professor and director of the Change Program for international managers at IMD, the International Institute for Management Development in Lausanne, Switzerland.

Index